Transforming Childhood

A Handbook
for Personal Growth

Strephon Kaplan-Williams

Journey Press
1988
Berkeley, California

ACKNOWLEDGMENTS: To Terran Daily and Linda C. Beam, both of whom did separate text readings with comments and suggestions for change. To Luz Mena, coordinator for getting the book into publication and assisting with text editing. To Noah Potkin, for putting in text corrections. Thanks also to all the participants in the Transforming Childhood Workshops™ over the years. Without your participation we would never have known how healing this material is. Front cover design by Stanley Chan. Special appreciation to Dr. Elizabeth B. Howes for spiritual development, and to Dorothea Romankiw, for pioneering work with disturbed young people.

CAUTION: Working with this material may evoke strong responses, in which case seek skilled therapeutic help. Use at your own risk.

TRANSFORMING CHILDHOOD TRAINING: Workshops in Transforming Childhood with Strephon Kaplan-Williams and other trainers are scheduled in various countries, both for participants and those wishing leadership training in the process. Training in Jungian-Senoi Dreamwork is also available. Membership in the Jungian-Senoi Association, an association of professionals, is available to those who have graduated from our training. For more information please contact:

Journey Press
P. O. Box 9036
Berkeley, CA 94709

Other books by Strephon Kaplan-Williams,

Transformations I (1979)
Jungian-Senoi Dreamwork Manual (1980)
Seed Bursts (1985)
The Practice of Personal Transformation (1985)
Dreams and Spiritual Growth (co-author) (1985)
Sources (1985)
Changing Your Life (1988) formerly titled, *The Practice of Personal Transformation*

First Printing: Oct. 1988, 3000 copies, 100 signed and numbered.

_____

Forward

*in warm appreciation
to*

Luz Mena

*only she knows how great
a support she has been
to my work
of reaching the world*

When I think of the word, "transformation," I think of a deep reconditioning that will allow a fresh new form. Although *Transforming Childhood* did not make me a new person after reading it, it engaged me in a process of transformation that continues to renew my life to this day.

I first read *Transforming Childhood* five years ago as the written class material for the course "Transforming The Myth of Childhood." The course was offered by the Jungian-Senoi Institute and was led by Strephon Williams.

I wondered if this course would teach me something new I could use in my life. I had taken psychology classes in school, and had studied childhood psychology on my own when I substituted six months for a prekindergarten teacher. This knowledge had been useful in my understanding of human behavior, but had made little difference in my personal growth. After working with the *Transforming Childhood* material I understood why.

I now know that intellectual knowledge alone will not get through my defense system. I developed this system while growing up to protect my vulnerability. While this system protects me, it also keeps important information about myself subconscious, and prevents me from growing. At times my intellectual ability is itself a part of my own defense system. No wonder it will not make a dent in it!

With the first *Transforming Childhood* lesson we were to visualize ourselves whole and balanced before we were born. For me the vision was almost impossible to sustain even for a few seconds. But having felt whole for one second encouraged me to commit to the course. The subsequent lessons went right through my defense system. They are written to do so by evoking a whole range of feelings as they help the reader reexperience early life situations. In working with the lessons I learned to help my old childhood wounds heal and to strengthen my choice-making process inhibited during my childhood.

Strephon welcomed our participation in class. He did not try to persuade us to agree with him. He did encourage us to look at the source of our disagreement. Did it come from our "Center"? Or was it a reaction to a threat to our defense system? As a rule of thumb I learned that whenever there was a lot of emotion behind my disagreement there was an internal issue at stake I needed to look at. If I still disagreed after working with this issue, I would simply move on. Strephon was not teaching us a doctrine, but a way to work with issues and to live life as a process of wholeness.

Having made the idea of "life as a process" a principle to live by, I tried not to look for results each time I worked with a lesson. But there were a couple of obvious results I noticed. I learned to recognize and attend the Wounded Child inside me each time she surfaced, and how not to let her destroy a dream I may be working for. I learned to let my Wondrous Child free as a source of spontaneity, and to recognize others' Wondrous Children to play and create with. I also began to relate to my family less as daughter No.3, or little sister, and more as my own self. By doing this I discovered them as individuals as well.

There is a long string of small changes I have experienced in the journey I began with *Transforming Childhood*. I probably could not identify all of them at this point, but I do know they have brought much growth and very special people to my life. I encourage you to join in working with this process, which has meant so much to me.

Luz Mena-Schrade

Preface

I can look forward to the publication of this book with a good amount of joy now that it is complete. In viewing the back cover I like to remark to people, "Isn't it amazing that a three year old could write such a book," referring, of course, to the picture of myself at age three. In a sense it was the child in me which did in fact come up with this material. I am the product of a terrible childhood and years of therapy, spiritual studies, and eventual transformation. When I devised this material several years ago my purpose was to organize for myself and others the process which had happened to me in fifteen years of Jungian analysis. This plus ten years of specialized training in the field led to my becoming a therapist/analyst in the Jungian tradition. But this material has roots which go beyond the traditional Jungian. We emphasize also experiential process, the major contribution given to the world by California and its consciousness movement.

Many people have received good results from working with the approach, so I know it works. My way of developing material is to write it up and test it out in actual in depth and ongoing workshops. My commitment is to both working directly with the process and writing it up in usable and inspiring form for others.

My passion for the Transforming Childhood Process™ comes as much from my own work and transformation as it does from working with others. I was so mixed up as a young man that I had little hope for a better world or for being a fully functioning vital person myself. My despair seemed infinite at times. I had only to look at the world, my friends, and my parents to see how difficult it is to live in a healing and conscious way. *Transformation can happen when we know the process and are committed to it.* My hope is that you as reader and respondent will also benefit deeply. I know a few of you will also want to contact me personally to share your own experience as well as to take workshops and further training in the work. Together, then, we can make our significant contribution to healing ourselves and the world around us. This possibility brings me joy and meaning. I honor your journey as you honor mine.

Strephon Kaplan-Williams

Berkeley, California, September 11, 1988

Table of Contents

The Myth of Childhood

Image: *once upon a time*

"Our goal is to truly graduate from childhood."

We all have a story in us called The Myth of Childhood, which is to say that we are formed at least in part by patterns developed in childhood, and which still rule us in adult life.

A few years ago I threw over the chess board when I made a stupid move in the game and my wife check-mated me. I was having an attack of the Wounded Child archetype. My wounded boy from the past was expressing his feelings. I felt cornered by a superior force and my inability to deal with it. This happens so often in our lives. There we are in some so-called "adult" situation and our inner child pops up. This is caused by conditioning from the past.

Parents abuse their children and their children grow up in turn to be hard on their own children. The family neurosis can be a terrible legacy to pass down from generation to generation. We fear it. Many will only go back to childhood because they are driven there by a desperate attempt to work out their problems. We return to childhood to face the original trauma and transform it.

On the other hand, your inner child may show up at just the right moments. Your are feeling frustrated with a friend or lover and you just laugh and mimic the absurdity of the situation. You have a paper or a letter to write and a new way of saying just the right thing flashes into your mind, recalling that spontaneity you most certainly had as a very young child. Or you are out on a first date and several things you do are a little wild, a little off, and you wonder where that is coming from. You just wanted to have fun that night, didn't you? So did your inner child, perhaps reacting to a rather stuffy or serious person you were making contact with for the first time.

And what if you want to have children but are afraid to because your own childhood was so rough? Your own wounded child archetype lurks just around the corner for you to run into in the darkness of your heart. Until you face your own long lost childhood you will have a hard time wanting kids of your own.

We also return to childhood to find the joy which comes with fulfillment based on healing. No matter what the trauma, there is the possibility for healing if we can somehow commit fully to the process of inner transformation as well as outer change. For this, we need guides and sign-posts along the way. This book is full of guide-lines for exploration. A lot can be done by responding to the information in these pages. Reading helps, but making changes is what brings in reality.

The Child and Parental Archetypes

There are woes enough in this existence, but before they turn you off to the valuable work, consider this.

That the source of creativity is the Wondrous Child, as the source of healing is the Wounded Child. That our full creativity and destiny can only come out when we are deeply in touch with our Child and Parental archetypes. That there are wonders to behold still in this adult world. That we can return to childhood, not just to suffer, but to find renewal there. That in our intimate behavior we can play, we can be instinctual, be creative, as well as deal with our garbage.

All longing for paradise is a longing to return to the lost childhood we never had. Do not project your longing for a perfect childhood with perfect parents into the sky, into an after-death experience of paradise. Live the transformed life now by integrating paradise within your own soul.

Childhood

We were born into this life, into a certain environment with a certain set of parents. But living deeply within our psyches already were The Father, The Mother, and The Child. We started whole. We had personality dynamics called archetypes. Unfortunately what happened to most of us was that the archetypes within us became only partially fulfilled. If the father is absent our "inner father" will not develop fully. If the mother plays the father role our "inner mother" will be broken. If the Child Archetype we are living out as a child gets attacked by the parents, as it often does, then the archetype may undergo a split into the Wounded and the Wondrous Child. The parents play the power game with us, trying to dominate our own development, they cause us to identify with the Wounded Child. We will still experience the Wondrous Child, but we may have to go into fantasy to do it.

In other words, from a harsh childhood we learn to withdraw.

Even if we had an easy childhood we may still feel lost or not understood. The natural parents will only be able to constellate certain aspects of the parental and child archetypes. We carry deep wounds into adult life.

The greatest wound of all is not having the archetypes fulfilled in the actual experience of life. Thus we enter the adult world physically ready, but hardly able to function psychologically as adults. We enter adult life and marry our parents. The archetypes seek fulfillment, we mate with our peers, and in the new bond seek that which we did not realize in our first childhood.

Adult relationships are themselves the second childhood. Not many grow up in their own life-times. They may have jobs, raise children, become old together, but the symptoms are there in childish and dependent ways.

Consider all the compulsions, alcoholism, the dependency syndromes, the governments run by power-hungry, booze-drinking men and women? The disease is not even alcoholism, for beyond that, the compulsives suffer from an unresolved childhood. No one is self-destructive or destructive of others who has resolved their own childhood.

Need we mention all the split relationships and all the relationships which have lasted too long? If we have not solved the dependency problem we have not become adults. If we have not solved the dependency problem, we are, like most of us, adult children caught irretrievably in the Myth of Childhood, the pattern that keeps us immature.

Our long-term goal is to leave childhood by integrating the Child and Parental archetypes inside us, rather than projecting them outward onto parents, lovers, authority figures, God and Government.

The Process

Our process is a simple one based on direct experience. Using the chapters in this book you will cover major archetypal experiences of childhood. By reexperiencing any of them now, working with the material and the questions, and doing the exercises suggested, you will enter into a deep transformational process. You may also want to work with a therapist during this time, attend workshops, do dreamwork, to get added support, or you can also form a support group in which all members work with the same material together and share their experiences.

You will not find a strictly chronological sequence to the chapter-lessons. The Myth of Childhood is not chronological as it was the first time around. Think of your myth of childhood as an organic set of impressions forming a loose pattern, a crystal of many facets which you go in and out of with your expanding consciousness. As you make progress, a growing sense of the whole will develop which is not linear but circular around a common and moving center. We must break up the old rational ways to find a new vitality.

Statement of Purpose

We return to the childhood experience to find the traumas and splits. We reexperience these again, but this time within a healing context. We want to heal the archetypes by bringing out aspects not yet actualized or made conscious in us. We want to discover the larger pattern for our lives, and seek to fulfill it in a wholeness process. We want to live with a strong ego, a choice-making base, and also serve the larger process of the Self, the central archetype of integration and healing. We want to live the child in a non-compulsive way. We want to learn to parent ourselves without projecting out and seeking parental figures and situations. We want to find our true work in the world, and also have fulfilling relationships. We want to be centered in all that we do.

The Parents

The natural thing to do once we have contacted within us the hurt and anger repressed from childhood is to blame our parents. Yes, they were imperfect, one or more of them may have abused us, or neglected us, or been too hard on us, or not understood us, so wrapped up in their own big worlds were they. So we blame, we see the oppressor outside ourselves and do not look at our own self-defeating parts. But blaming others, and sometimes ourselves, does little in the way of helping us cope with life. No one is to blame for anything. Reality exists just as it is and you can do nothing to change what actually happens to you or anybody else. The facts of experience are irrefutable. There is no one to blame, to make wrong in the situation. When the results are in, it is too late to change their cause. The only redemption of the past is to act differently in the present. All you have is what is occurring now.

Until we have accepted our childhood just as it evolved we will be seeking causes and assigning blame. We will be hostages to fate. While we cannot change what is happening to us, we can change how we relate to what happens. This is the crucial point. Things always need to improve, to heal, everywhere. But healing comes through action, not assigning good and evil to the experiences of life, thereby rejecting one and accepting the other. To graduate into adulthood is to accept the whole and deal with it as creatively and courageously as you can while evoking the healing sources of life at the same time.

Graduating from childhood has little to do with your actual outer parents if you still have them. The only way to do it is not to change your parents but to change yourself. Your myth of childhood is inside you and this is where you must work. You cannot forgive another person for what they have done. That would be arrogance since it would imply that you have special powers. *You can, however, evoke healing for your own inner parents and children and thereby experience forgiveness yourself.* As you change, then your world will change with you. Do the inner work and the outer will change as well.

What the Myth of Childhood Is

The Myth of Childhood is the inner behavioral pattern created in actual childhood to express ourselves in adult life. We learned in childhood how to cope with fundamental experiences and how to retreat for survival. We built there a defense system to deal with potentially overwhelming forces. We had experiences of God, or a healing power, which perhaps we could not get others to understand or accept. We encountered adversarial energy in ourselves and others. We developed ego, learned self-identity. So many things happened to us. We developed and then entered the adult world.

Each of us has a story of what childhood was like. This is also our myth of childhood. It is based on selective memory and how archetypal dynamics were constellated within us. What we do now with the Transforming Childhood process is to rework the myth we developed so that the pattern can become whole, the wounded can be integrated with the wondrous, so that we can move into being a centered and effective person.

We can transform our myth of childhood. People who have gone through this process have an inspiring story to tell, and a new life to live. They will be living from their own centers rather than living governed by the original childhood material. This is a great accomplishment, one of the finest achievements possible in this life-time. You can live and die still a child, or move fully into adult life. You have that choice.

The picture we have of childhood is the picture we have of adult life.

§§§

How To Use This Book

Image: *the journal lies open—tears and laughter*

"To become free we must reexperience the past on an inner level."

The exercises in these lessons come out of much healing work in practicing Jungian analysis, a process of helping persons re-orient themselves to their own wholeness process by working through childhood material as it is still affecting them today.

We suggest that you work with the book either in therapy, in a small group or class, or on your own. What is possible is to take one chapter or lesson a week and respond to various questions. Some of the questions you will do thoroughly, some not at all. Write your responses in a journal and then share them in a small group or with a friend or therapist. It is even conceivable that a whole family can work through the book together. What an adventure that would be! If you feel overwhelmed by your material, please seek competent therapeutic help.

Methods for Transforming Childhood

In order to feel secure in dealing with childhood material as it comes up, we need to have methods for integrating the material. One of the chief methods we use is journalwork.

In journalwork we assume that much material from the unconscious can be understood and processed without having to necessarily act it out. What is essential is that we let ourselves be moved by our own experience of the archetypes in an inner and feeling way.

In letting ourselves be moved by what is being evoked, we are often reliving aspects of childhood at an archetypal level. We are not actually reliving a childhood experience, although it may feel like it.
We are reliving the mythic pattern in our psyches originally created in childhood by our natural disposition, our parents and other influential people, and by the events themselves. The reliving is the re-experiencing of the archetypal pattern so that it may be changed, and so that we are not unconsciously dominated by it in adult life. Our goal is to free ourselves from the past to function creatively in the present. To become free from the past we must reexperience the past on an inner level. To become free is to take back projections originating in childhood which we put onto people and situations in the present. As adults it would be better not to go around projecting our inner child and inner parent onto our friends and authority figures.

Another value for working at an inner level is that usually we can deal with the material evoked in small enough increments so as not to be overwhelmed. Journalwork, and our other techniques, serve to process what comes up. Acting out repressed energy in the outer can lead to explosive situations which make us retreat or repress all over again.

The final level of the process is to relate the material and the changes which have taken place at an inner level to the choices we make. We move into the outer from a firm base in the inner world, where the archetypal patterns and unconscious ego-controlling attitudes lie.

In summary, you will be learning a way of working towards individuation, a wholeness process which can be applied to any area of life, dreams, relationships, and other material from one's unconscious. Our goal is to become more and more inclusive of the different elements of life by creating a growing ability to process whatever comes our way, inner and outer.

To process is everything!

§§§

The Methods

Image: *the vegetables lie nicely chopped on the cutting board*

"Your journal is the true story of your life."

The Journal

A journal is a blank book in which we write our private feelings and experiences. A journal is not a diary. In a dairy, we are focused on recording a historical narrative of our lives. In journalwork, our focus is to process the energies of life by writing about them, often in a free-flowing, non-structured way. In journalwork, we are mostly concerned with the inner and consciousness producing aspects of an experience.

Basic structures to the journalwork might include dating the entries and giving titles to most of what we write. Creating titles for things is a way of helping to realize their essence. Other structures might include researching and summarizing your journal entries separately in order to create further direction from the material.

It is often best to make it clear that you want no one to read your journal without permission. If an intimate insists on reading your journal, try to get them to start one of their own. You must have the freedom to put anything you feel down on paper. Having to censor material is inhibiting to the psyche. We have enough social strictures in the outer life. We need to be freer at the inner level.

Your journal is your friend and confident. Writing in it will also relieve you of the need to continually discuss everything with others. You will become less subject to others' influence and more contained and integrative as a person. Your journal is the true story of your life.

Specific Journalwork Techniques

Free Flow Writing • This is the way to write most journalwork entries. You have in mind the subject you are going to write about. You feel excited by it. But you do not usually organize how you will say it. Instead, just let the words come out. You will find that almost always you write beyond your known point of view about the subject. You may also feel a sense of resolution or moving on about the problem. Date and title the entries, and work quickly and in a place where you cannot easily be disturbed.

Dialoguing • This is a form of free flow writing in which you choose a part of yourself, or some energy, to have a conversation with. If, for example, you are upset with a friend, you might first go to your journal and ask the image of the friend why you feel so upset with him or her. You ask the question and then write quickly, without censoring, everything which comes into your mind. Then you might follow with another question or a feeling of your own. And so it goes until you feel you have arrived at a resolution or you have gone as far as you desire to. Such a dialogue often gives us another point of view. It opens us up to other sides of our selves and even gives us information we may want to reject. In other words, we discover what we are projecting onto a situation or person and own it as ours. This increase in consciousness often has a resolving effect in our outer world as well.

The Unsent Letter • This technique is often a powerful one and, therefore, reserved for special occasions. Perhaps there are things, often angry things we would like to tell another person which might be dangerous or not appropriate to say. Or we may simply feel too afraid to say our true feeling in the outer. To our rescue comes the unsent letter. In it you write as if you were sending it. You write everything you wanted to express but thought you couldn't. Such an experience can have a freeing and resolving effect, and if truly felt, it will be as real as if you had actually sent the letter. Once having gotten your feelings out, you may want to send a modified letter, more delicate and appropriate, but one still stating your position on an issue. The principle is to get the feelings out, no matter what, and this is a fairly safe way.

Writing Poetry • Poetry is the language of feeling, and thus can be used to express feelings which cannot be stated appropriately otherwise. For instance, if we are experiencing intense love feelings for another person who does not reciprocate, we can still write beautiful poetry to our love object which expresses our own feelings. More often than not, we do not give them the poem. To write it is enough for getting the feelings out. The journal receives our poetry and thus we do not give ourselves away. Poetry is expressing feeling in imagery and thought. Journalwork poetry does not need to conform to any literary structures. Let it flow straight from the unconscious without fear and without focusing on approval or public appreciation.

Dreamwork • Recording dreams with titles and dates can also be part of one's journal. After the dream report, it is helpful to write down comments. Comments may be questions or feelings about the dream, but not rational interpretations. To get to the meaning of the dream we may use various methods for re-experiencing it, which are illustrated in the *Jungian-Senoi Dreamwork Manual*. Sometimes it is possible to make connections between one's dream life and outer life. Dreams often mirror the dominant archetypal energies moving in our psyches at the time.

Describing Outer Life Events • Certain events in our lives will have special significance for us, such as starting a new relationship or job. What is important here is the energy generated by the event. If I am in bed waiting for sleep, thinking over something which happened in my day, it would be important to write about it in a free flowing way until I have arrived at the essence, choice, or issue involved. The goal is to process, not to merely describe. I have experienced something. What is its significance? What is its possibility? What is its danger? What is its value?

Active Imagination • Active imagination, or meditative reentry into an experience is excellent for re-experiencing something and bringing it to resolution. We close our eyes, become quiet within ourselves, and focus on or visualize the experience. Once the flow of imagery and feeling gets going, new things which we had not anticipated may develop and move to a natural resolution of the issue. After we have lived a certain experience, we then write it down in our journal and perhaps comment on its meaning. This is often a powerful technique because, in effect, we are entering directly into our archetypal patterns, and through experiencing them, we are helping the patterns shift and become viable again instead of static and blocked. The danger is that sometimes we can become lost in the experience, and this is why writing down and processing the experience is necessary. Naturally you should not evoke more than you feel you can handle. Taking things in small doses is usually enough.

Changing Attitudes • An attitude is a context out of which we make choices. Often attitudes are unconscious and can be expressed as a single sentence. "The future is likely to be worse than the present" is an attitude many of us have. Such an attitude, when not consciously realized, would cause us to make choices to avoid change and stay with the status quo no matter what. In any situation we can observe carefully how we are acting and search for the attitudes which motivate the action. Then, once articulated, we can refashion new attitudes to be more reality oriented and less life-defeating. It is not enough to make attitudes conscious. We must also work to change them. Values are attitudes consciously realized. The more conscious we become the more choiceful we are, and the more fully and meaningfully we can live life. Once having formulated a new attitude we work with it as an affirmation. We say the new attitude to ourselves and we try it out in life by making an intention for action out of it.

Art Work • From time to time in order to enhance or symbolize some energy we are dealing with we can color and draw in our journals. We are not after literal representations or beautiful art. We want only to express the energies moving in us to the best of our abilities. It is important not to negate oneself by aiming towards something one does not do well. The journal is a journey receptacle, a safe and accepting place for processing the energies of life and the psyche. Use it well.

Therapy and Analysis • Therapy may be needed if the material you are working with seems too evocative and more than you can safely handle. Going into therapy gives you support and insight in dealing fully with your material. The goal of most therapy is to become self-processing and integrative. Much of what we do in class or in our journals is also focused towards that end. But for especially intense experiences, or because one wants to work as deeply as possible, therapy and analysis may be the choice. Analysis differs somewhat from therapy in that it is usually long term and deals with levels of the unconscious not dealt with in therapy. Therapy provides support for dealing with the more immediate issues of life, as well as for becoming effective.

Supplementary Reading List

Changing Your Life, Strephon Kaplan-Williams, Journey Press

> This book is a chief reference work since it has detailed methods and background on working with the dynamics of the psyche, such as choice-making, attitude change, anger, love, and so on.

Jungian-Senoi Dreamwork Manual, Strephon Kaplan-Williams, Journey Press

> This work offers a complete and practical dreamwork approach necessary for those readers who choose to follow their dreams at the same time they are working on their childhood material.

The Inner World of Childhood, Francis Wickes, Appleton

> This classic goes in and out of print in paperback. Look for it in used book stores. It is excellent.

The Drama of the Gifted Child, Alice Miller, Basic Books, Inc./ Harper Colophon Books

> This also is a classic whose main thesis seems to be that much is done by adults to limit the natural growth of the child.

The Origins and History of Consciousness, Eric Neumann, Routledge & Kegan Paul

> This is the great Jungian work on the emergence of consciousness out of childhood into adult years.

The New Diary, Kristin Rainer, Jeremey Tarcher

> The best book, despite its title, specifically on journal writing, written with a sense of creativity and ease.

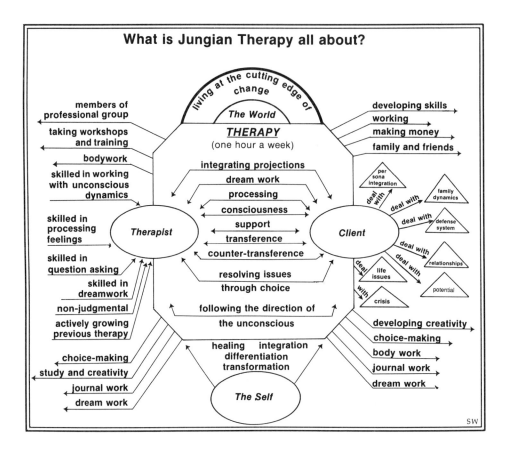

What is Jungian Therapy all about?

living at the cutting edge of change

The World

THERAPY
(one hour a week)

members of
professional group

taking workshops
and training

bodywork

skilled in working
with unconscious
dynamics

skilled in
processing
feelings

skilled in
question asking

skilled in
dreamwork

non-judgmental

actively growing
previous therapy

choice-making

study and creativity

journal work

dream work

Therapist

integrating projections

dream work

processing

consciousness

support

transference

counter-transference

resolving issues
through choice

following the direction of
the unconscious

healing   integration
differentiation
transformation

The Self

Client

developing skills

working

making money

family and friends

persona
integration

family
dynamics

deal with

deal with

defense
system

deal with

deal with

life
issues

relationships

deal with

deal with

potential

crisis

developing creativity

choice-making

body work

journal work

dream work

SW

Beginning The Journey

Image: *the vessel*

"…what alone is effective is a re-membering that is also a re-experiencing." C. G. Jung

"It is of course impossible to free oneself from one's childhood without devoting a great deal of work to it…. Nor can it be achieved through intellectual knowledge only; what is alone effective is a remembering that is also a re-experiencing. The swift passage of years and the overwhelming inrush of the newly discovered world leave a mass of material behind that is never dealt with. We do not shake this off; we merely remove ourselves from it. So that when, in later years, we return to the memories of childhood we find bits of our personality still alive, which cling round us and suffuse us with the feeling of earlier times. Being still in the childhood state, these fragments are very powerful in their effect. They can lose their infantile aspect and be corrected only when they are reunited with adult consciousness. This "personal unconscious" must always be dealt with first, that is, made conscious, otherwise the gateway to the collective unconscious cannot be opened. The journey with father and mother up and down many ladders represents the making conscious of infantile contents that have not yet been integrated."

    C. G. Jung, *Psychology and Alchemy*, p. 62.

This passage lays the groundwork for all that we are to do. In it are the keys to dealing with childhood. These bits and pieces are of primary importance in dealing with our own psyches. Jung emphasizes here the integration of the lost parts, the childhood survivors living deep in our own unconscious. If we do not reveal and integrate these parts they will cause infantile behavior in us as adults, the clinging dependencies, strange moods, and general failures in maturity. Childhood, which one would think is to be an experience of growth and preparation for the adult years, turns out to be also an inhibitor of maturity, a liability we take into adult life. We must heal the neglected parts of ourselves as well as integrate them.

What also needs emphasis here is that we not only have the childhood story we believe in, the myth of childhood, the list of traumas and delights, but we also have the unfulfilled myth of childhood. We can return to childhood to heal, to complete the archetypes first experienced there. The end result is that what we add to Jung, to his emphasis on the trauma, is the vitality of the archetypes in their fullness. We seek the Great Mother and Great Father. We seek the Wondrous Child as well as the Wounded Child. Then upon "graduation from childhood" we will have made real a new myth. We will have found the lost parts, the full archetypes which were only partially constellated by our actual parents. We will have found life.

The Work

Respond freely in your journal to any or all of the following questions designed to help bring out the meaning for you of the above passages. There are no right responses, of course. What the questions stimulate for you as you listen to yourself is what becomes real. Write freely.

• What does it mean to free oneself from one's childhood? Why even attempt such a task?

• What for you is "a remembering that is also a re-experiencing?"

• Why are the memories of childhood important?

• What would it mean to have childhood content lose its infantile effect?

• Why must we come to terms with and know our personal unconscious?

• What is an actual experience to go with your response to any of the above questions?

We journey on by going back to the beginning.

§§§

The Grandparents

Image: *roots exposed above the ground*

"...somehow I had been taken to the door of my heritage."

The first and last time I met my grandfather on my father's side, the old man was ninety-six and I was thirty. Two days after my father died I was taken to see my grandfather by my father's brother. He shook my hand when we met and then briefly left the room. My uncle had said a few words about me in Yiddish to the old man which had to be translated for me. When grandfather re-entered the room he gave me a twenty dollar bill and took my hand again. I was quite moved, not by the money, but by the acceptance he seemed to be conveying towards me. The recollection of this man and this event will burn in my soul forever. I left feeling that somehow I had been guided to the door of my heritage. By this simple act I had been given the family blessing which only an elder can give. My grandfather was one who had survived a kidney operation in his own thirties at the turn of the century. Only one out of six living at that time made it through having one kidney removed. What spirit moving in this man's veins moved also in me? I wondered. With this gesture, with his blessing, I could and would do much in the world.

The Work

• What feelings were brought out for you in reading this passage?

• What is a blessing?

• In what ways did you receive, or not receive, a blessing from your grandparents?

• If not a blessing, what did you receive from your grandparents?

• Perhaps write a letter, which you do not send, expressing your feelings about a sense of received blessing?

• Perhaps you could make a four-fold diagram illustrating what each of your grandparents symbolizes for you?

• We may have learned a far greater sense of time from our grandparents and other family ancestors than from any clock or calendar. Write about your own sense of "destiny time."

The past parents us with wisdom as the future parents us with new life.

§§§

Our Parents As Children

Image: *ducks floating on a pond*

"Children often make the best parents."

Let us go back in time to those years before we were born. Our parents probably did not know each other then, and they were living with our grandparents most likely. As a society and a world, the environment on the material and spiritual plane would have been radically different.

Yet here we are today wondering what of that past we are still living out in an unsatisfactory way. What attitudes and values did they have which would have been appropriate then but are quite unsatisfactory now?

Picture your parents as children. What did they have to contend with? What legacy, positive and negative, were they given which they tried to pass on to you when you were a child?

I am convinced that the most universal of themes running through all childhoods is that tendency of parents to project their own repressed and otherwise unfulfilled childhood expectations onto their children. In this very real sense we were all parents to our parents' inner child. We found ourselves in a fundamental conflict between bringing up their unresolved child and affirming and expressing our own natural child, the person we were meant to be.

What then is it that we most have to forgive our parents for? Obviously the traumas and neglects, but perhaps most cogently for the enormous amount of time and effort spent in trying to make of us the child they always wanted to be and never were. The only real wound that any of us carry is the wound of lost life which can never be gained again and therefore must be given over as a loss into the fires of redemption. The irony lies in the realization that what the parents tried to give us in their own best expectations was in fact a loss for us.

Perhaps we feel we never conformed to the parents' expectations by rebelling against the pressure. Yet even while we created distance, in the unconscious we remained as tied as ever. We remained tied in reaction rather than conformity. The true freedom is to find ones own individual way, the way from the natural child to the adult we were meant to be.

The Work

• What am I holding on to that I haven't forgiven my parents for?

• What is one of the most vivid images of my parents' childhood? What images of my parents as children do I have? What inner image of parent inside me does this evoke?

• What are some attitudes towards life that my parents may have developed as children?

• Visualize yourself holding your parent as a child in your arms. What feelings are created?

• Were your parents forgiving or not forgiving of their parents? In what way has this affected you?

• Describe how you might have been the parent to your parent's inner child.

• In what way could you still be parenting your parent's inner child today?

The child is parent to us all.

§§§

Our Evolutionary History

Image: *a luminous dark sphere shadowed with light*

"You are not yet born, yet something is already here, an immense complexity, a miracle of billions of births."

Picture it yourself.

Before you were born the great organism, life, was already here on this planet. Each one of us is made up of actual molecules, the same type of basic units of matter which also helped compose other living creatures centuries and centuries ago. We exist with a consciousness built out of tens of thousands of years work and experience by *homo sapiens*, man and woman.

The legacy of what we call life is in us today, but is far more than we as single individuals can be. The whole evolutionary history of who we are exists now in each of us, and yet together we are one great organism living, moving, changing on this earth in order to produce the essence which will evolve the next generation a step further along than we are at present.

Think of it and marvel. How petty our troubles are when we consider the immensity of the achievement which is ours to live today.

Will we embrace life and make our contribution to the whole?

You are coming to this planet which already has life. You are not yet born, yet something is already here, an immense complexity, a miracle of billions of births. You are but one potential in many, you will be arriving soon. Think of it. You will be next someday.

What will you bring with you? What will you find already here on this planet earth? What will you contribute by the time you exit life?

The worlds are spinning closer. Welcome what will soon be your ground, your resting place, your state of manifestation. Welcome the great essential we call life!

The Work

• Read the paragraph over, perhaps out loud. Let yourself feel it. Go into meditation or visualization. Be there somewhere in the universe. Who are you at this point? What are you coming to?

• After your experience, please write it up, giving feelings, images, etc. and responding to the questions embodied in the text.

• List the possibilities which come to mind as you begin to feel the spark of what could be and enter into a journey of receiving a body which is born and goes through childhood into adulthood.

• And, of course, list any hesitations, resistances or questions you might have. After all, part of you might not want to be born.

To evolve is to step through time into time.

§§§

The Conception

Image: *the flame has left its fire*

"Self born of what and born to what?"

In an instant something of you was present somewhere, somehow. In the dark warm depth of human flesh a whole lot of energy was at work expanding itself and gathering in.

And where was soul, that infinitesimal spark which is neither flesh nor energy? The moment of essence into being must have been the moment, indeed. Nothing begets nothing and something is born. What great rivers of life and destiny met in that uniting which your parents made and created together in their time of pleasure?

Seen from a more cosmic viewpoint, two great energies had their meeting, the masculine and the feminine, and out of that coming together the Self was born. Self born of what and born to what?

Not all seed reaches an egg. One does and the penetration is done. Swift multiplication follows, matter quickens within incredible possibility. And clinging there to warm and nurturing flesh, the wall of womb, the supplier of what it takes to become. The cost is everything. The commitment is total. There is often no turning back.

The Work

• How would you describe the moment of conception as you think it happened for you?

• What was the nature of your parent's union? Was it spontaneous and joyful, or ambivalent and strained? Were they united in spirit as well as in flesh?

• What effect, if any, do you imagine the quality of your parents' union had on your entry into life?

• How would you describe the two streams of life which came together when your parents united, conceiving you?

• How would you describe your soul, or spiritual essence, at the time of your conception? Just let go and describe. We are admittedly reaching into the unknown, not for literal facts, but for archetypal flow.

• How would you describe your womb environment those first days of rapid growth.

• Do you in any way regret being conceived? Do you have any regrets about the union of your parents that conceived you? What are they?

We are conceived within the womb of time to break out into eternity.

§§§

The Womb

Image: *the fisherwoman has caught a silver fish*

"Limitation is true freedom"

Something happened to you back then when you were still in the womb. What was it? Try to recall.

Or if you wish to remain in the present, ask yourself, what is the womb of your life right now? How do you deal with constriction and any narrowing of your personal freedom? Do you rebel and kick and try to fight your way out? Or do you accept your fate and go with whatever is happening to you?

Are you womb-cursed or womb-blessed?

Somewhere back then in the deep recesses of the bellied womb of flesh of your mother, you met and dealt with the first closing in on you. Picture yourself in the first three months of growth, a floating ball in the warm pond of your own amniotic sack. As you grow you reach the walls, the natural restrictions which are the structures of your own mother's womb.

You must curl and almost contract, yet continue growing, continue pushing out at all sides so that you can continue to manifest yourself. And the pushing and the stretching become more difficult, until one day the walls of your life began contracting and you find yourself being squeezed out.

How well do you take restriction today? Limitation is true freedom!

The Work

• Visualize yourself in your mother's womb. Take a few minutes with eyes closed to let go to the feeling and possible images. What is the experience like? How are you responding?

• What is your personal history of becoming dizzy? When does it seem to happen? What feelings are evoked from becoming nauseous? What can you do about it? What change of perspective is needed?

• What areas in your present life need containing? What is containment and how does it work as a process?

• What relation to the womb experience might commitment have?

• In what ways could limitation be true freedom for you? How can limitation free you to become yourself?

The womb of commitment is the place for new birth.

§§§

Birth

Image: *the chimes are ringing in the square*

"I choose to be here."

Return to the womb. But this time come out kicking, screaming or dancing, or gazing at the world, taking in all that is. Come out and be willing to stay out most of the time. Let us return to birth to right the balance and to choose life. Did our birth make us defensive or energized?

And how well do we allow and work for the new births in our lives?

I love the agony of birth because I know the world waits for me. The world waits to challenge, nurture and support my being, my person, my time in this existence. And I in turn?

I choose to be here. I choose to want the birth with everything I have, including my regressive pull. And I am here because I am wanted! If not by my parents, then by life. Life created me. Life welcomes me in joy and in pain.

The Work

• How would you describe what your birth process was like? How is it similar or different from my present change and growth patterns?

• Go into a meditative state for about twenty minutes, let go, and let images and feelings come out of a focus on re-experiencing your being born into the world. Describe everything and then write it down. List what got evoked for you. Perhaps later check out with your parents what actually happened at your birth.

• Then after doing the above, or at a later time, go again into a meditative state and experience your ideal birth. Let this birth experience be as healing as possible. Then write it down and list what was evoked for you.

• Write up how you typically wake up each morning. Then write out your ideal way of waking up and the values to be gained.

With each new birth we wake more to life.

§§§

Choosing Your Parents

Image: *a tree split open by a great force*

"We must accept what happens to us rather than resist it."

We come into this world a mere speck of flesh and a spark of soul in somebody's body. We have not chosen to be there. Our mother and father have sex and the sperm and egg have came together to produce the me that is I. Did I want to be here? Did I ask to be chosen? Did I have any choice in the quality of the parents I received? Was this all accident or is there some destiny in it?

If you would ask me why I chose my parents I would first say I had no choice in the matter. But if you would press me to reflect further I would have to reply, yes, I must have chosen those particular parents because no one in their right mind would have given me the people I got. My choice-making was strange indeed. Certainly God could not have made such a choice, so I must have made it myself.

Why did I choose my parents?

I wanted to make life difficult for myself. I came into the world as a very strong person to have given myself such difficult parents. I was sent away to boarding school at the age of six because they both decided that they were not fit to be parents, and that poetry and art were their only devotion. To compound the event, I was told by my father's girlfriend after my mother's death that he said he had not had sex with my mother for the first ten years of their marriage, and that I was an accident.

So I must have chosen my parents riding a stream of destiny so strong that it demanded of them to have sex. I look on in disbelief at the precariousness of life. It might just as well have been someone else who was born in our place but somehow we were meant to be here.

No matter the tragedy, or the goodness of childhood, we can face the question, why did I choose my parents? Why those two? What was the necessity to have those parents? The transformation of childhood is the acceptance of childhood just as it is. I discovered in therapy rage at what had been done to me, but what could I do but express it and let it go? Childhood was over for me. I had only the charged and tragic memories. These also I would have to work through. For to hold on to the tragedy of the past is to remain blocked to the future as well.

One great lesson of life is to accept rather than resist what happens to us. I would have preferred better parents to the ones I had. But now, years later, I have gotten over my rejection of them. They are my parents, quaint, abusive, but essential to my destiny. I do not want someone else's parents as I did in my youth. There is a peculiar, wonderful quality about these parents of mine.

I have accepted reality.

I have chosen my parents.

The Work

• Why did your parents choose you? Write about it, please.

• Why did you choose your parents? Write freely about how you played a part in receiving the parents you got. What is it about your particular set of parents which is necessary to the fulfillment of your own life?

• Why was it necessary for you to be born? Why is it necessary to live?

• Create a little humor about the fact that you were born to the parents you got. Tell someone about it, or act it out a bit for a group.

Through choice we turn fate into destiny.

§§§

Nurturing

Image: *her breasts are bare*

"No one will give us all the love we feel we need in this life."

How well and how fully were you nurtured, fed, and warmed after your birth? While suckling on the full breast and clinging to the ground of your mother's flesh, what stability and openness were born there?

Or was it more the opposite for you? Did you experience yourself taken away or deprived of the breast and the holding? Did you experience also the void and the coldness of the Dark Mother, the Great Mother of Deprivation?

> There is a photograph of me as a baby in diapers standing on my mother's lap. One of her arms steadies me while the other arm and hand hold a baby bottle. My mother is well dressed and sophisticated. My down-to-earth aunt, her sister, is also in the picture, as well as my girl cousin. Obviously my slim mother did not define herself as a breast-feeder and so I missed out on some essential nurturing. I know now what it is like to suckle on a warm woman's breast, to feel secure in letting go to a basic need, to experience the relief of someone actually being there willingly for me, someone who enjoys giving to me. What a fight it must have been struggling with that bottle, my first civilized tool to manipulate, cold impersonal thing that it was even if the cow's milk was warm within it. I had to learn in adult relationships with caring women that nurturing was not something you could manipulate to get. I had to become the vulnerable baby again before she could give freely to me. At first it felt humbling. Now I experience it as a natural letting go to receiving and pleasure. I am receiving. I am being nurtured by something real!

Return to the present, take this moment as the Womb of the Now. How fully do you give and receive nurturing? Are you a compulsive seeker of nurturing? Or a compulsive giver unable to receive? If so, what unfulfilled needs from childhood still hide in your unconscious?

Most adults seek and express nurturing in relationships. But what may be crucial is to become more and more self-nurturing to oneself.

No one will give us all the love we feel we need in this life. The answer is to love! And to love oneself.

The Work

• What feelings are evoked for you from reading the above passage?

• What questions from the above would be important for you to respond to? What is your response?

• Enter a meditative state and feel-imagine yourself at your mother's breast. How long can you stay there and experience whatever comes up? What is it like? Write about it.

• Look at your present relationships in terms of the wish to nurture others. Explore ways this can be done and the values and consciousness involved.

• Look also at your present relationships as places to be nurtured, to let go to warmth and acceptance, and to be fed.

And we shall be nurtured by choice, not plenty.

§§§

Bonding

Image: *a bird flies into the sun*

"And in love-making, are we not again yielding to the primal bond?"

Bonding is the mandala, the completing and breaking of the circle of life. We are born and immediately we seek to cling, to be reunited with the mother-flesh, the nurturing warmth of the primal source out of which we so recently came. And in love-making, are we not again yielding to the primal bond? So many of us find it hard to let go of a relationship when it has ended. The beloved is again the parent and we are again the child. We are required by reality to leave the mother bond but we fight it. We are afraid to be alone, to exist solitary to ourselves.

Witness the toddler child of one and one-half moving a room away from the parent and then hurriedly returning. Leave the door open, Daddy. Don't break the bond on me.

In life we bond to all sorts of things. We bond to our cigarettes if we are a smoker. To our lovers and friends for support. To our work and our jobs for security. Life is all so simple when we look at it from a child's point of view. But as adults we are not here to live a child's life, at least not all the time. All experiences of pleasure, in fact, may be in some significant way a return to childhood. The adult needs the primal experiences but does not need to be bound by them.

It sometimes takes willingness to step through the fire. The tiny child crawls away from its parent to explore the world. After all, there is more than mother in life. But should the distance feel too great and the bond too thin, then the child cries out to be reunited with its parents. It has gone forward but retreated again. And so it is with us adults. We need the warmth and renewal of the bond to the love object. But we do not need the attachment. It is good to have little attachment left by the end, to become individuals with the parental dynamics inside us. We then have the primal bonding in us as a healing circle in which we are integrating all our parts. The inner family is alive, and as adults we do not need to compulsively seek primary bonding in outer family or groups. We are individuating. We are developing wholeness within.

The Work

• With your eyes closed see yourself as a small child relating to a parent. What bonding pattern shows up? How does this pattern also assert itself in your present life? What creative choices might you make regarding your bonding pattern?

• If you at times feel isolated and cold, what are some conscious ways you can experience bonding with some source of renewal? Explore creative bonding experiences which are not self-destructive or compulsive. Compulsive eating, sexuality, drug taking, talking, smoking, etc. reflect unconscious bonding behavior. Loving someone, relating to animals, having massage and bodywork done on you, etc., are more conscious ways to find renewal through bonding.

• Also practice unbonding from compulsive needs. Use your will to break compulsive habits and deal with the anxiety which is evoked. Give yourself so much love and affirmation that the compulsive need to bond will diminish. The overweight person is often one who feels afraid and incapable of being loved or bonded to. Gorging on food becomes less compulsive when we love ourselves and become feeling-sensitive to our bodies. Loving our bodies means feeling and healing them.

We can bond with others if we have formed a healing bond within.

§§§

The Baby As Body

Image: *the walled city has some houses on fire*

"We must therefore liberate the body as well as the soul."

The body is where we live. It is the house we inhabit. But how many of us totally accept this house we carry with us? It is the source and bedrock of all our adventures. We cannot escape it for very long. This body of ours has a language of its own. We need to come to terms with where we live.

The baby is being born, the baby is having sensations within the womb and then out of the womb. What care does that helpless body receive immediately and in the future?

Babies have bodies. Bodies need plenty of touching and hugging and having needs met. Bodies need food and flexibility. Immediately the body has needs of its own and the baby cries out. But even at the start so many parents oppose the natural rhythms of the body . Feeding time four times a day. Let the baby cry. Be afraid to carry the baby around with you everywhere.

The new baby who receives plenty of physical attention will grow up with an attitude that its needs can and will be met in a plentiful world. Strength comes out of being given to, as well as from from giving.

The list is long of all the major body experiences we go through as a child. Birth... breast or bottle feeding... bowel movements... falling down and experiencing pain... eating... defecating... being washed... masturbating... hugging... experiencing anger... seeing oneself in the mirror... male and femaleness... sickness... vitality and high energy... feeling others with warm bodies also.

So much of early life is felt through the body, and then in the adult years we experience all sorts of physical symptoms as we deal with the stresses and changes of life. It is as if each one of us has had our bodies rigidly patterned to act in set ways to life's problems. And, like so many things, the original patterning was formed early in childhood. Watch for it. When do I become sick and what kind of sickness do I get?

Much sickness, from the serious to the mild, from allergies to cancer, from the common cold to flatulence, are due to the original body-reaction pattern formed in childhood. The remedy? Try consciousness and change. Discover for yourself the original pattern producing the present symptoms. Do practices which restructure the childhood reactive pattern to a more natural and vital functioning. This is why every one of us could gain from extensive bodywork of one sort or another. Have we been held lovingly enough as children? Are we trying in adult life to make of sex the healer for the traumatized body it was never meant to be?

A basic premise flows through all the childhood material. We are our bodies. Our symptoms in adult life are evoked by contemporary stresses, but their origin is in the original body-reactive pattern formed early in childhood. We must therefore liberate the body as well as the soul. We must liberate the life force physically as well as mentally.

The Work

• List the typical body symptoms you regularly suffer in adult life. They do not have to be major, and can include such simple things as backaches and warts. Now for each symptom associate, or let flow, early childhood memories and images. What are your earliest experiences of having a body? Write these down. Let things flow freely.

• Draw a body chart of yourself and at various parts of your body. Place on it the symptoms you have or now suffer from. Where do you seem to feel most vulnerable? Where are the areas of greatest vitality? Write steps you will take to deal with the symptomatic parts of your body, such as exercise and other forms of healing.

Your body is reality.

§§§

Waking

Image: *a ball of fire growing in intensity*

"What is done in the beginning sets the course for what comes after."

The way we wake up each morning can be the way we were born into the world, whether we have a memory of that first entrance or not.

Consider your life and how you start your day. Do you wake eager to experience the newness of each day? Or do you tend to return to sleep as the much preferred place to be? Why face the world any sooner than we have to? The warmth of the bed and the unknown land of the unconscious may seem preferable to the suffering, excitement and choice-making of an active day. Do you jump out of bed into the day's activities too soon, or do you take a few moments to savor and acknowledge the transition between sleep and waking?

How many of us wake each morning eager to face and fulfill life to the utmost? How many of us bring with us into the day a dream from the night, making transition from the world of moon to the world of sun? If our transition is poor from sleep to waking, chances are that the transition from mother-womb life to separate life in the world was difficult and abrupt.

And so it goes. Many are afraid to fall asleep at night and eat anxiously before bed or read a book. Then once they fall asleep they have to fight to arise, they have to have a jarring radio or alarm clock wake them up. Truly, their basic life patterns were traumatized at birth and still affect them daily in waking life.

What would it mean for each of us to wake slowly each morning capturing a dream or a significant thought or feeling? What would it mean to wake refreshed and eager to leave bed and deal with the joys and trials of a typical day? It is crucial that we begin each day at the beginning, not somewhere partly down the road. What is done in the beginning sets the course for what comes after. If you are not starting each day significantly, look at your present sleeping and waking pattern and create a more fulfilling one. Each day that we wake fully and consciously is a day in which we transform a little more the traumatic entry of our original birth experience.

It is time. It is time to wake up. It is time to get it together, to grow, to change, to become vital. It is time. Choose and move!

The Work

• What exactly is your sleeping and waking pattern? Describe in detail and then relate it to how you feel you were originally born. Do you wake inwardly focused or outwardly focused? Do you wake thinking of a dream, or some outer task you have to do that day? Or do you wake resistantly, wanting to hide or go back to sleep?

• In what ways have you woken up to life and its meaning? In what ways might you still be asleep?

• What does it mean to wake up to life? Ask this of yourself and a few friends this week.

• Write in your journal for a week on how you seem to wake up and the changes you are making in that pattern.

Those first must sleep who would awake.

§§§

The Pain Of Childhood

Image: *the tree's branch has been broken*

"We are not yet mature if we always seek pleasure over pain."

"Johnny, you shouldn't hit Tommy. That's not good."

"Janie, be nice to your younger sister. She loves you. It's not nice to yell at your sister. See, you made her cry."

Behind each of these typical statements used in child upbringing are certain attitudes.

- It's wrong to hurt people.

- The right thing to do is make people feel good. You would want them to do that for you, wouldn't you?

Who gives us these attitudes? Do they come directly through us in our own wisdom, or are they imposed on us from outside? The answers seem obvious. The reality of the situation is that children in their natural state fight as well as play together, inflict pain on each other as well as make each other feel good. And what do parents do with their children? None of them would consider it good behavior, but all parents cause pain in their children. If they could only admit that they are inflicting pain as well as pleasure in their children, the parents of the world would become a lot more realistic about life.

Pain is here to stay. We have pain receptors built into our bodies just the way we have pleasure centers. We are taught to avoid pain and seek pleasure, but is this a valid approach to life? Perhaps, just perhaps, there is just as much to learn from suffering as there is from pleasure.

Where our training in childhood goes off is in being taught that pleasure, the good, the socially acceptable, the pleasant, are all of value, while pain, suffering, weirdness, wildness, rebelliousness, are all roundly condemned as being bad.

Is it any wonder that we have not been trained to deal with the difficult side of life? We have been taught to repress the bad in favor of the good. Look to your own past. What was your earliest experience of pain? What brought it about? Were you taught how to deal with it?

A new mature attitudes regarding pain is that, pain is as valid as pleasure in living a meaningful life.

We are not yet mature if we always seek pleasure over pain. There is pleasure when the life force flows freely, when we feel healthy, when things are working well in life. There is pain when the life force is being blocked, when there is resistance to change, when things are unbalanced or needing to be destroyed. Pain is also the effect resulting from the challenge to let go of the old and bring in the new. If these statements destroy a few attitudes, let them. If you are angry now or agitated, it may be because some of your own attitudes are at stake. Let go and go with. Learn from the new even if it embodies the dark side of life.

In compassion we can feel the overwhelming pain we must have felt back there in childhood. We are all born into a rough life, and somewhere the "wounded one" lurks waiting, hoping to be rescued. Yet nobody comes. We must leave our hiding places ourselves and go out to where healing and truth can occur. Yes, there is an infinite well of sorrows, and sometimes my own hurting dips down into a universal despair. This makes me very sad, but my sadness is real. I welcome the pain of being real. No, I am not always happy and don't need to be. Wholeness is better than happiness any day, and when my pain comes I will be ready for it.

I know that within pain are the fires of my own transformation.

The Work

• Return to the most painful experience of your childhood and write about it. What you will be doing is accepting pain as a natural ingredient of life that originally you closed off to. Now open and let it happen.

• Work with pain in your life, not as "pain" but as "energy." Energy is the sense of movement within and without which creates new life. You feel pain. Focus on it directly. Find it in your body, seek images from it, look at your reactions to it, and above all, recall early childhood memories and attitudes which now relate to your pain. Pain immediately plunges us right back there into childhood.

• List your attitudes around pain. Revise each one to make them more realistic and inclusive of the wholeness principle.

There are things which only pain will teach us.

§§§

Anger

Image: *the well has been blocked*

"It takes energy to repress energy."

We are only ultimately angry at ourselves. Even though it feels like we are angry at everyone else who has ever hurt us, ultimately the anger we feel is our own.

We become angry when we feel powerless and vulnerable to being hurt. Normally, our defense system prevents negative energy from getting through to our consciousness. But every so often someone "presses our buttons," the attack penetrates our defensive pattern, and repressed energy sizzles us to the core.

It takes energy to repress energy. To protect our wound we become angry, and to ourselves protect our self-image, we repress the anger. This causes an energy drain which devitalizes us and creates depression and despair. Thus by freeing and transforming our anger pattern we free the life energy from the defense system. To free our anger we first identify the defense system that may be keeping us from experiencing it. Then we express our anger. Anger is one of the two great instinctual forms of energy expression, the other is sex.   Finally, we transform our anger by allowing ourselves to feel the wound underneath it. We must freely experience the ecstasies of suffering as well as of pleasure.

Now let us look at the nature of our defense system. At some point in childhood we chose to hide our emotions and feelings from ourselves, and others. We were confronted with the overwhelming power of the parents, other significant authority figures, or a traumatic event. We could not take it, so we constructed a defense system to hide from ourselves and to deny the full impact of reality.

As adults this defense system no longer works as well as it worked in childhood. In fact, it imprisons us from living fully. We may deny aspects of reality, space out, identify with archetypes, roles and religions, rationalize feelings, repress feelings, avoid intense situations and the next life developments. You name it, we have all done it under the aegis of protecting ourselves.

What is there to protect ourselves from? It is all life. Reality is what exists, so why not encompass all of it?

We return emotionally to our myth of childhood simply because that is where it all started. We go back to the traumas and grand hurts to face our adversaries, to reexperience these events emotionally without closing off this time. By suffering through the trauma without becoming completely defensive we will be helping the underlying patterns and attitudes to transform, so that we may regain our life energy and direction.

Yes, it's painful. But pain is an energy that one can learn to handle. Suffering exists and is essential to life, so why not accept it emotionally and create with it?

The Work

• What was your anger like in childhood? How is it similar to, or different from, your adult anger expression?

• Try and describe a wound experience, where the pain became too much in childhood. Relive it at some level using journalwork. Perhaps you could write it out. Or write unsent letters describing your feelings. Or paint the scene? Or keep telling friends about your trauma until you, yourself, have accepted it?

• How would you describe your defense system in terms of anger? Write an affirmation accepting your own anger. Formulate an intention to express your anger more creatively.

To wield the sword you must first draw it from its safe scabbard.

§§§

Witches

Image: *the tree is hollow*

"… the God he feared was a Woman."

When I was a child in boarding school, we would spend the summers in the school camp far away in the woods. It was always a highlight for us eleven year old boys to receive twenty-five cents and take a hike all day to the honey man. We climbed and ran through the forest and then descended by a dirt road to a small wooden house-shed which still had a water mill wheel working in the stream. This "white witch" was an old man surrounded by his swarms of bees and his many bee hives. He seemed stooped over, not from suffering, but from being some sort of guardian of the waters and caretaker of the bees. To us he was magic, and therefore to be feared. Bees meant danger as we ran barefooted through the fields of wild flowers. But this man who lived alone had some influence he could use to make bees give their best.

We each paid our twenty-five cents and received a whole honey comb for our very own. The "white witch" was for me the one who knew nature and who had been molded by her. The price he paid was his old age, and the gain he received from his worker bees was the elixir, the sweetest, most powerful essence of natural life.

The world itself was a lot duller the next day. But something beyond the everyday remained in our imaginations forever. The White Witch had created in small, growing boys a fearful and excited respect for the natural forces of life.

I had my terrible witches also. My own mother was one, brooding in bed when I came home on short vacations each year. Those gleaming eyes hid their sadness, but revealed all too well a wildness to the young boy, myself. This woman held immense power over my mind and destiny, and I learned slowly to placate her where I could. Alas, she followed me into my dreams and secret thoughts, terrorizing me for years. She was to me the dark witch, the one familiar with evil who used it on me and justified her every action. I learned from her the truth, which she herself did not seem to face, that there is no escape from the pain of consciousness, and that the darkness of the night is too often laced with despair.

Now, I know her to be my mother, old, neurotic Gene Derwood Williams, who had been in the mental hospital for a year when I was three.

The Work

• What feelings, or moods, are aroused for you by this passage?

• Why not describe the experience of a witch in your own childhood? Witches seem to represent the magical, sometimes evil and sometimes nature-power side of things. What effect did your witch experiences have on you back then?

• In present life, see if you can recall an experience of a witch, someone with numinous, or archetypal power, over you. This might be a person or a dream personage.

• Now for the clincher. How do you express, or not express, the witch side of yourself? Look for the more irrational and bizarre behavior which yet has a strange logic, a secret meaning, to it. Perhaps this witchy part is a peculiarity of your own mental state or consciousness? Could that be?

• What do witches add to childhood?

For renewal open the door to the irrational.

§§§

Fear

Image: *the mouse's tail sticks out of its hole*

"Only the ego feels fear."

So you are afraid? You don't know what to do and perhaps want to run, to hide, to feel safe. Safe from what? From the Great Adversary? From life itself? There are so many things to be afraid of in this life. Life is so hard, so full of suffering and difficulties.

Yet why fear anything at all? All that is out there is life itself, life to be lived to the fullest, life which includes the good and the bad, the creative and the destructive. Life, I love every part of it, its danger and destructiveness as well as its warmth and happiness. May we all be given life in equal measure, the great opposites themselves.

But none of us start out that way. Do we? Are children more open to life as it is than adults? Certainly open children live more fully than closed adults. Life is for living. Therefore, I am for all of it. Give me the whole thing or I will not do well with any of it.

Some of us are still rejecting certain parts of life as stupid, evil, awful, and so on. Those with the greatest fears seem to do the most rejecting of life. Where I fear there also I reject, and in rejecting I am missing important aspects of life.

Only the ego feels fear. And what is fear? When I perceive the possibility of my own annihilation, I feel fear. I am afraid when I perceive I may lose something, even my life. When I feel fear it may be important to take measures to protect myself, or others, or things which I deem valuable. But at times to be identified with anything in this life, even one's own soul or body, can cause us to withdraw fearfully into ourselves and avoid the adversarial aspects of existence.

What we identify with is what we most fear to lose. Adversity is that which opposes. Some event or force comes into our lives and loosens us from whatever we are identified with. Our health, our money, our job, relationships, a way of behaving, values, needs. If at these times of challenge I contract in fear, trying to hold on desperately, I will not have the flexibility to make the necessary shifts in consciousness to better deal with the situation. Rather than contract in fear, open in the face of challenge, go through the fires of your own transformation and make the necessary shifts to cope with a changing reality. Fear lights the way to possible danger but must never itself be allowed to be the danger.

What was I as a child afraid of? Falling down and hurting myself? Losing my parents? Being rejected by others? Having things I held dear stolen from me? Getting attacked and bullied around? The list is endless. Did everything I fear happen to me? Yes! Obviously, being afraid does not stop the adversary from regularly entering my life.

It is not what goes wrong in life which is to be feared, but fear itself. Fear is that which can contract us and force us to choose retreat and inadequacy. If you want to be with that man or woman, go after them. You may fail. You failed many times in childhood and still made it, maybe barely, into adult life. You will fail, and you will succeed, but only by leaping the barrier of imagined inadequacy. Life is what comes your way when you actively choose it.

The Work

• What were the things you were most afraid of in childhood? How did you deal with each of them? How do they connect with what you are afraid of now? What are your successes in dealing with fear and its inhibiting and anti-life quality.

• Describe your fear pattern and how you can bring choice to what you go through.

We fear what we most need.

§§§

Playing The Power Game

Image: *children riding up and down on a see-saw*

"The frail little bouncy baby must assert its power."

What we are most afraid of is our own annihilation. Somewhere back in youth our parents, siblings, or society, tried to win the power-struggle. They sought to dominate and make us do what they wanted. They used power to physically, or verbally, abuse us. Poking at children, calling them names, hitting them, invading them, teasing them, are all attempts to act strong by making the other person weak.

Thus the source of child abuse is the perpetuator's own feelings of inadequacy. But most parents practice child abuse to a certain degree. Anyone who invades another's life is at the edge of abusing them. Parents who ask their children countless questions may be abusing their children by making them "tell all." Other parents come into their children's rooms when they want, or read their mail, listen to their phone conversations, read their journals. These "milder" examples still illustrate the invasiveness of parents who often assume that they have a right to know and inspect their children's inner lives. The effect of such behavior on children is to weaken their sense of boundaries and self-identity and to make them withdraw or fight back in sometimes secret and manipulative ways.

Because children are smaller and dependent for shelter, sustenance, and caring, they must compromise with the environment in which they are forced to live. Immediately they find that others are not always there to meet their needs. All babies cry when they are in pain. Their suffering usually causes the adults to act, to hold them, to feed them, to give them love. This is the baby asserting its own power, for it knows instinctually that it is already in competition for the attention of the adults. The frail little bouncy baby must assert its power.

But some adults do not respond, turn off, leave the baby alone in its crib despite its screaming, or hit it to shut it up? Most parents have had these thoughts, and some act on them. The insecure adult may start trying to win the power game, may try to dominate the baby in its struggle to have its needs met. Inside, the adult is, in repressing the child, repressing his or her own wounded, inner child. How sad!

Somewhere in childhood those with power might have defeated you, drove you into yourself where you hid out. They won the power game. They did not practice the great and valuable principle of "balance the power, do not try to defeat it." Meet the child's needs, but in a way that you can meet some of your own needs as well. Let the child win sometimes. Let the child develop into a strong individual by encouraging self-assertion. Only come in and oppose where safety and strong values are at risk.

In the adult years if you act out the childhood manipulation pattern you developed to get your needs met in a family where parents practiced a power struggle, you will be defeating yourself. You can learn to ask for what you need in order to get your needs met directly. You can be with people who do not try to win the power game over you. And you can recognize when you attempt to force your way through others' needs in an attempt to meet your own.

Being overwhelmed by someone playing the power game against you can also be perceived as fear. Learn to cope with fear by taking action. You can seize the initiative and stand up for yourself. Develop your own power and balance energy with anyone else who comes your way. You can do it. You can begin to do it now by acting with directness and using the power available to you.

The Work

• What are your attitudes around power? What childhood experiences helped create them?

• What was your earliest experience of being overwhelmed, or almost overwhelmed, by someone else's power? What defenses or manipulation pattern did you develop out of that? Are they in effect today? If so, how can you transform them?

• In a meditative state go back into an early childhood trauma of being defeated in a power struggle and this time keep asserting yourself, equalizing somehow the other's force. See what finally happens. You will be changing a pattern inside.

• In the next month be aware of situations in which you lost your power to another out of fear. Rehearse what you could have done differently, and keep rehearsing until you have built a habit of asserting yourself in a sometimes adversarial world.

• Practice balancing the power in every situation and see what it evokes for you. Trace feelings and attitudes back to childhood where appropriate. Create new attitudes and self-images of someone who is usually able to balance power with power.

The twin measures of power are meaning and effectiveness.

§§§

Rejection

Image: *a refrigerator door found washed up on the sand*

"No one can reject us but ourselves."

Everyone seems to have a rejection problem, from the most traumatized to the most supported in childhood. Rejection is then a problem for the ego to deal with, a problem inherent to the ego's dynamics.

No one can reject us but ourselves. Yet we go around afraid of the Big No, afraid that someone will reject us. People can say "no" to us a million times in this life, but no one can reject us unless we reject ourselves.

Unless we negate ourselves, we cannot be negated by others. So why this fear, this apprehension that I will not get what I want or need? If we identify with a negation we will be subsumed under its power. If I am afraid of the "no's" in life, I will not risk trying to get to the "yes." To not risk experiencing the fullest possibilities in life is "The Great Negation."

Why wait for the best to be handed to you without any intention or effort on your part? Chances are you will wait forever. What I need is what I ask for. What I ask for generates what I am likely to get. What I get, no matter how unexpected or contrary, is what I need, and what I need in life is to affirm its fullest potential.

Go back to childhood still another time and experience there your first great rejection. So what! It was time for your next lesson in the game of life. But did you learn it? Or are you still depriving yourself in the way others deprived you? We reject ourselves because others have rejected us.

And today? Today I will begin a total program. Today I will not reject myself by saying "no" to my desires before anyone can say "no" to me. If you can take "no" for an answer, you can ask for anything.

The Work

• List some ways you still cannot take "no" for an answer. What is the pattern or gut feeling underlying it all? How well do you say "no" to other people? If you have a problem saying "no," list some possible attitudes and feelings which may be behind this inability.

• How is not saying "no" to others actually saying "no" to yourself? Did you think that you could escape saying "no" in life?

• List some things you will ask for in the coming week, and list also after each one, how many "no's" you will accept before you give up trying to get what you want.

• What is the biggest "NO" you are afraid of? How might you reduce it in size? What was the big "no" your parents gave you? What "no" would it have been good for your parents to have given you?

• Write up an early childhood experience of rejection. Write the attitudes embedded in your description. Write up the effect of this experience and resulting attitudes on your behavior today.

• What is your rejection problem? And what is its possible transformation?

• Visualize your ideal parent accepting you fully. What is the interaction? How do you respond?

We reject the possible for fear of the impossible.

§§§

Speech

Image: *leaves falling endlessly from innumerable trees*

"We talk to hear ourselves."

No sooner out of the womb, nay, while still in the belly of the mother, the baby cries, and gurgles in pleasure. We are born to make sounds, to affect others around us. We are born to convey the measure of our experience. Speech is the second birth.

Unfortunately as we became adults the words and sounds of our mouths become as tired as old branches falling. We do not say what we mean. We complain about life. We talk it out and often go on living the same old way. Our words have lost their integrity, their ability to change us or others. Why?

This is what many of us learned in childhood about speech.

> • We learned that words did not matter. It was the actions which counted.

> • We learned that we could say only part of what we thought. We had to begin censoring our words, thus causing a split in our personalities between the part we could show to the world and the hidden often more true part of ourselves.

> • We learned that the adults did not listen to most of what we had to say. The adults did not understand us and were selective about what they wanted to hear.

> • We learned that we were to tell the truth, but we saw that the adults lied to each other, described the facts about our own person differently from the way we perceived them.

• We learned that it was safer to lie or not say anything in order to protect ourselves from adult power used to dominate us.

• We learned also that the grown-ups wanted us to say everything which was on our minds but that sometimes they would use that information against us. They would embarrass us in front of our friends, punish us for wrong-doing. We gradually learned to keep our mouths shut with the unfortunate results that we felt alienated from others and even from ourselves.

• We learned that talk was dangerous. You had to learn to say the right thing or you would upset someone. We learned that we could not say what we felt because no one could take it, not the adults and not most of our peers.

So as we grew up to be adults, our speech became degraded. Now we must redeem it. If we do not express ourselves we will not express life. All words express something essential about life. Although some words seem good and others seem bad, they all have their places as expressions of reality.

Some of us use talk as a verbal masking. We talk non-stop about ourselves, not allowing pauses in the conversation for silence, or for the other person to respond. We are preventing intimacy by controlling the verbal impression the other person receives. As mature people we can learn to heal our tongues. We can learn to say what we mean, give voice to what we feel, listen carefully to others, articulate the language colorfully, and use it to be effective in the world.

Others say little but think much. They are afraid to express who they are and hide behind the mask of silence. They need to learn to put themselves verbally out into the world, to share themselves and to give up alienation and unbonding.

Verbalizing is a reflective process to make conscious what is happening to us. First we live the experience, and then we reflect upon it, trying to find the meaning in what we just lived out. Most of us talk our lives through with others. We talk to affirm our life and consciousness, to convey value and experience to others. We listen carefully to make contact with another person, and to change. To fully hear someone is to let their words affect you. If you leave from an in depth conversation unchanged, you have not heard what was being said. Talk, then, is the interweaving of inner content with outer reality, the healing bridge which cures alienation, and which brings the joy of living to the world.

The Work

• What are some of your earliest memories of speech as a child? What seems to be reflected in these memories about yourself?

• What was your childhood talk pattern like, and how is it still in effect today? Use the text above to analyze how you did or didn't talk. How is this pattern still active today, and what can you do about it?

• Were you honest as a child? What kind of lying did you do? Where would you lie today? What does lying do for you?

• What commitments can you make as to how you use speech for growth and direction in life? Examples might be, to say how you feel no matter the circumstances, or to express what is going on inside you at various times throughout the day.

• How did you express yourself today using words? What are some ways you might become more expressive and real in the use of words?

• Practice listening to someone else and resaying some of what they say so that you may practice accurately perceiving another person's thoughts and words.

• To free up your language for more feeling responses, practice talking in imagery. Let go to your unconscious and let the images come. Also give personal reactions to what you say. This is the feeling response.

Hear what you say and you will say what you feel.

§§§

Regression

Image: *the toilet bowel has flooded over*

"…every regression… is an attempt to return to childhood… "

Oh, I don't want to get out of bed today. I'm so tired and basically lazy.
And so it goes. Sometimes life seems so hard. I'm an adult now. I have
responsibilities and an image of maturity to maintain. But what hard work
this life is! Leave me alone, will you? I want to regress a little.

The regressive pull is a mighty force in our lives. We have all these goals
and things we have to do, but somehow we can't quite get going to do
them. We should be growing and productive all the time, but it never
works that way. Two steps forward and one step back, sometimes one step
forward and two steps back.

Creative regression is to consciously slip out of our known adult
personality, the images of maturity with which we are identified, and slide
back a number of years to earlier behavior. Some of us are so identified
with our adult personas that we find it amazingly difficult to consciously
choose moments of creative regression.

"I'm going to rest now, I will let go and have some fun. I'm not going to
do anything today, nothing! The whole world can go to hell as far as I am
concerned. Let's play and act like little animals. Wouldn't that be fun?"

If we do not consciously regress from time to time in order to escape the
adult persona and find renewal, regression will take over when we can
least afford it. Sickness will strike when we need to be well. Sleepiness,
spacing out, losing things, drinking, forgetting, the list is long of
unconscious regressions we do in order to find renewal. But unless these
ways of regressing are brought to consciousness, we will remain at war

with ourselves.

Creative regression can take us back to that place of the child, the original spontaneity and creative flexibility for life. Take moments throughout the day to just let go of everything, like a two or five minute nap. Allow yourself to be playful and act like a child where appropriate, or nearly appropriate. A momentary laugh may be a letting go.

We are re-experiencing our childhood again in order to live it more fully and bring it to completion. One of the results will be that we can more easily let go of our adult persona and find renewal in the inner child. So, in effect, every regression, planned or not, is an attempt to return to childhood and can be dealt with as such. Love the child and let go a little or a lot!

The Work

• What are your typical forms of compulsive or unconscious regressing? Describe them and what might evoke them. Define creative alternatives to meet the needs causing these regressions.

• In what ways were you too mature when you were young and therefore missed being a child? What aspects of being the child have you not had a chance to live fully? Everything? Pin down what you missed the most. How might your present regression pattern be influenced by this?

• List creative ways you might regress a little during your day to find renewal.

• Write a positive statement about yourself which includes your ability to regress. "I am good at regressing..."

We lose ourselves to find ourselves.

§§§

The Family Archetype

Image: *the forest on the mountain burns*

"Many make the choice to preserve the family at all costs,"

The family archetype, unintegrated, is a motivating force in many of the difficulties of adult life. Most of humankind go to their graves never having become conscious of themselves because they remain in the family archetype.

Examples of the power of the family archetype over adults include the following. Living next to one's parents all one's life. Calling parents "mom" and "dad" in adult life instead of addressing them by their names. Married people calling each other "mom" and "dad" is another extreme. MOM and DAD are not real people but archetypes, symbolic primaries without individuality.

To graduate into adult life we must break the archetypal hold which inner and outer parents have on us. If we cannot call our parents by their real names at least some of the time then we keep ourselves identified with being a child, a form of dependency. We also do not do our part to help challenge "mom" and "dad" to become real persons in their own eyes regarding us.

Does one need to give up the family in order to get free of unconscious domination by the archetype? Most of us certainly must liberate ourselves physically and psychologically in a number of ways. But wholehearted rejection of the family is not the solution because no matter how far we run, the childhood family stays inside us until it has been dealt with. In solving the family problem we will become free to better relate to the family as an inner and outer experience. We can become more loving because we have extricated ourselves from the prison of the archetype.

Can we individuate, or follow our path, and achieve inner wholeness within the family?

The forces causing us to play different roles within a family system are so powerful that it may not seem possible both to individuate and put your family first. In childhood you tried to become yourself and look what happened. The family attempted to break and claim you for its own. You needed to resist to find your own being and way.

Yet individuation is possible for a family as well and its members. This would take an open family structure in which all members seek to balance power rather than give it away or grab it, and in which members share and process everything which comes up.

The family image of the future will be one of wholeness, of nesting, fertility and relationship which creates new life, one that creates out of itself the freedom to both journey alone and in company of those who are our true companions. We may leave the original family behind, but we will find others of like mind and heart with which to journey and achieve a common purpose in life.

The Work

• What is your position on calling your parents "mom" and "dad"? What do you think their position is? Fantasize what might happen if you told them you wanted to use their adult names in relating to them. If you have the courage, choose to call your parents by their real names and not Mom and Dad. Feel what this does for your inner growth.

• In what ways are you still trying to live your childhood family life in your adult primary relationships?

• How have you sought the ideal family in certain group experiences? How have you tried to work out your own childhood pattern in groups with authority figures? What failed? What did you learn about yourself and groups?

Wholeness without is only possible from wholeness within.

§§§

The Family Dynamics

Image: *the string is full of knots*

"Family dynamics… enable strange and different people… to live together."

You are back in childhood again. Everything that happened to you has a purpose, some lesson for you to learn. You were born into a web, and you contributed to the configuration of that web whether you knew it or not. You studied and played at how things worked in your family. Who was beholden to whom? Where were the points of power? You studied what you had to fear and what was only bluff, what you could get away with and what was dangerous to do. And you found where the power lay which was yours, yours because for the others in the family your power depended on their secret weaknesses.

Did you become your mother's confient, able to hear what would not even be told to your father? Were you in league with the old man, knowing how to ride on his hidden feelings? How did you manage to make your corner of the nest secure against the intrusions of brothers and sisters? And what did you do about the family shadow, the ghosts hidden in the closet, the neurosis passed from generation to generation which no one was willing to talk about? Did you choose, in fact, to break free of it so that your children would not suffer the same fate you did? Or do you still not have children of your own for this reason?

Family dynamics are those patterns established unconsciously to enable strange and different people, who call themselves a family, to live together. In order to maintain the pattern, we each give up something essential to our own being, we make the grand sacrifice as our contribution to the sovereignty of the family archetype.

Let us include in the family picture some of the more positive patterns and practices, like singing songs together, which give the family warmth and life. Our goal is consciousness. We want to choose and transform. We want to redeem that lost child who had to adapt at the price of not being able to become her or his unique self. At their best family dynamics support and make real major potentials as the individuals grow and change through life.

The Work

• A number of important questions have been raised in the above passage. Which questions do you gravitate toward? Create a full response to one or two, or all if you choose to take the time.

• Make a drawing of each of the members of your primary childhood family. After you are finished, write feeling reactions to your picture. Then describe the picture to someone else so that you may make conscious the dynamics in what you drew.

• Make a diagram of power in your family. Try to describe the different kinds of power each family member had. What was your kind of power?

• Write a description of you in your room, what you did there, and what kind of a refuge it was for you. What were you seeking refuge from? What happened there in your own solitude?

To find the pattern, find your unique place in the pattern.

§§§

The Garden Of The Heart

Image: *the wind has blown the covers off the bed*

"Everything had a place and a story."

Once, long ago, in a wonderful room somewhere lived a little girl, or was it a little boy? And in that room were many magical things which only little people knew about. And this place was known by the spirits which lived there with the little person as "the garden of the heart."

In the room was a bed and on the pillow of that bed was a small doll, or was it a stuffed animal? Or was it even a tiny being? It might have been anything in that rainbow room. All we know is that to the person who lived there many things were alive, not the least of which were the beings who lay on the pillow every day and night or sat on certain shelves in the room.

And there were books in that room, picture books and word books and old books and new books and books you could smell and books you could get a big person to look at and tell you a story from. And then one day you yourself could open the pages and hear the story inside yourself as your eyes moved across the page.

It was a room in which to be alone. Most of the time the big people would stay out of your place. They had rooms of their own they liked to go to. You could hide from the big ones and see pictures and tell stories. You could bring a friend like yourself into your own space, and he or she would know you through your room and make up stories with you about what went on there which nobody but yourselves knew about.

There was the secret of the bottom drawer, the secret of the tiny man who lived there and one could not see unless one looked very close, and even then you might miss him or be in danger of sniffing him up into your nose. You half suspected that you had sniffed up many little beings in your room because from time to time you had to sneeze and never knew why. You learned to aim towards the bottom drawer which you always kept open a crack just in case, and your mother never understood any of this and was always tidying up and closing the drawer on you.

Oh, there were so many things alive in the garden of your heart as you lived among your real people as you called them. Everything had a place and a story. Many beings talked to you and you hoped you were a good listener, and you always acted on what they had to say, and had to ask their permission before you could fall asleep at night.

And now so many miles and years away from that room all seems gone to you, an image out of the past never to be lived again. Can you see it floating away down to your left? Those rooms and companions you had in the old days seem to have faded, and in their place is the painting on the wall, the crack in the ceiling, the photograph at your desk, the clothes in the closet. When you are gone the ones that survive you shall come in and sort everything out. Some leftovers they will put in boxes, some in the trash. They will give some things away. But how will anyone ever know that secret world, the child's room and the adult's living space, how will they ever know what inhabited the garden of your heart?

The Work

• What did your childhood room mean to you as a child? Write about it and how it served as a focus for your life. What were your parents' relation to your room. What inside yourself represents your childhood room?

• Take a favorite object, doll, stuffed animal, etc. and describe it or have an active imagination dialogue with it. Ask it to give you a description of what you were like as a kid. How does this affect you now as an adult?

A true secret never survives the telling of it.

§§§

The Wondrous Child

Image: *the cocoon is laced with gold which the child holds*

"Find this lost child and you will find life."

This child exists somewhere, inside us. Perhaps we embodied him way back there in the beginnings of our childhood, perhaps we will see him personified in the physical child we will help bring into the world. Or we may only know the existence of this child by a near-silent ache somewhere. Most likely you have seen the child, when you saw someone's child do something which was absolutely right for that moment. For an instant, you felt what it could be like to be the child of life. It was your own inner child who gave you a glimpse of the radiance.

At the darkest time of the year, the Winter Solstice, we celebrate in this culture the birth of the Divine Child, another term for experiencing the Wondrous Child within us. At Christmas people act a little more wondrous, more caring, more joyful, more giving. The Gift, the archetypal symbol of life, is offered from the heart. For what is the great gift each of us receives if it is not life itself? What we do with this gift is our choice. At the darkest time of the year we make sacred the birth of the new light. Thus each year we seek renewal through contact again with the Wondrous Child archetype, that dynamic which represents new spiritual birth in our lives.

Unfortunately, also at the Christmas season many are afflicted with sadness and even acute despair. At that time the wounded child comes up instead of the wondrous child. People who cannot return home to family and childhood feel left out, lonely, on the edge of depression. And even within the regular families all is not always well. There is bickering, manipulation, and outright fighting, as the wounded child pops out trying to be recognized where the wondrous child is supposed to reign supreme.

The truth is that many parents unconsciously or consciously hurt or kill our wondrous side as children. We became identified with the wounded child and the wondrous child disappeared or hid out in fantasy. We entered adulthood repressed and too serious, and therefore unable to express wonder and joy on a daily level. We lost our sense of creativity, the mystery, the flexibility to grow and change, no matter what the circumstance. For the wondrous child represents in us that spontaneous creative dynamic which can respond to any situation with openness and freshness. As adults, if we enter a growth process we have a chance to face our wounded child and resurrect our wondrous child. We revive the happy child in us to get out of a repressed and compulsive childishness which refuses to let us become fully involved in life. We welcome the wondrous child in the joy which comes through conscious fulfillment of much that we are meant to be.

The Work

• Write a flowing description of your wondrous child. What was he or she like?

• At what point did that wondrous child get lost? What was the trauma? What defense system had to be built to protect what was left of you?

• Have a dialogue with your wondrous child. Ask what or how this child can come alive in you now.

• Recall some of your most vivid memories of experiencing children as truly alive and expressing a certain essence. What qualities for you are being expressed in these experiences.

• Write a description of an integrated family experience of Christmas, Hanukkah, or Winter Solstice.

The joy of being creates the radiance to love.

§§§

The Body

Image: *in two hands is cupped living earth*

"Truly the body is the vessel of love, not hate."

When we think of the body of the very small child, we think of vulnerability and diapers, of smiles and cries, of perfection and miracle, of smooth warm skin, of suckling and eating pleasure, and of all the amazing growth and pushing through of form which seems to take place daily. The body is perfect in itself in all its functions. Then why as adults do we hide and chastise certain bodily functions so?

Parents, quickly enough, socialize their new born and growing infants. Clean up the feces and urine. It takes time but we are taught to control our bowels and our sexuality. The urges of the body do not necessarily get met when the urge is there. Do not teach the child by right and wrong or disgust. Teach the child to be aware of the animal sides of himself and learn to be appropriate so as not to cause unnecessary anguish. But as you teach the small child, do not condemn him for being the animal he is. And as an adult have mercy on your own animal, the body which is you, which is life, which lives, grows, expresses energy, has wastes and dies.

The ego tends to identify with the body. My body is me. Yet who am I? I do not always feel in my body. Sometimes I may go for hours in some activity without realizing that I am in a body. Then I feel the physical strain, the urge to eat and defecate and I remember where I am.

And where am I? Was I taught in my early body control training to see myself negatively? If my feces or sexuality disgusts me then I am less likely to see myself in a positive light. I produce that stuff which is hard for others. I am the menses, the urine, the semen and the excrement. So there. I am a creator at all times. To live I must take in and give out. Do you then accept me? Do I then accept myself?

In sickness and in health. Was it hard in childhood to be sick, to feel that which was me, vulnerable and painful? Was I nurtured enough when sick? Or did I learn that to be sick was a hassle and that people only liked me when I was well? Or I only get attention when I am ill?

Return to the body. The great message for today's world is, Who is truly alive and accepting of their bodies? Would anyone kill another body in war and murder who knew truly the value of being alive in the body?

Truly the body is the vessel of love, not hate.

The Work

• What are your feelings around defecating? Write them out. Heal them by seeing yourself "taking a dump" as a kid and having a good time with it.

• What rituals do you have around "going to the bathroom." What is the control pattern involved? Or the releasing pattern?

• And now for your genitals. What were some early scary experiences around your genitals? What did you do? What was your pattern? What was your parents' response? Now for healing, see yourself as a child playing and having fun with your genitals. What is the value of your experience?

• Expressing sexuality or bodily waste involves our holding and releasing patterns. What is yours? Write it out fully. Then see where you can make some changes. Deal with the anxiety which results from this. That is new energy for life being released. Create with it.

What we love will love us.

§§§

Guilt

Image: *a dark-coned tornado*

"For guilt, substitute acceptance."

Guilt, an oppressive word, positive to a few, but to a great many of us an agonizing experience of inhibiting the life force. Most of us say we feel guilty, but what is it that we feel? Perhaps what we feel is tension, some conflict of opposing views and forces tearing us apart.

Guilt is the tension I feel between trying to meet my needs and living up to my or someone else's expectations.

In childhood the parents might have said that we should be kind to our playmates, and if we were not kind then we were bad children. But a child does not always feel kindness. A child may want to meet his or her own needs for possessing things or expressing anger and aggression. The child experiences a tension between meeting his own needs and conforming to adult expectations. And if the child follows his own way, he risks being judged as a bad child. Hence Guilt.

"I am bad because I put myself first before others."

Why feel bad because you did not fulfill someone else's need? And why make others feel wrong when they do not meet your needs?

To free ourselves from guilt, we must take the risk of expressing and pursuing our own needs and let others fulfill their own wants and desires. When needs clash, negotiate and compromise. In place of judging put actions and their consequences. It is not wrong for me to try and meet my needs first. It may be upsetting, and that is what I must deal with.

Whole systems of ethics and morality have been created to make us feel bad. If we go against the thousand and one commandments then we are judged a bad person. If we conform to collective values then we get rewarded by receiving approval and having our needs honored by the collective's power. To conform we must live in fear of doing the wrong thing and being disapproved of for doing it.

A creative way for dealing with needs is to encourage each person to express his or her own needs, and to work together for everyone's fulfillment. In order to do this new way we must give up judgment and blaming. We are not bad persons nor do we need to make anyone else a bad person. For guilt, substitute acceptance, embrace the differences, find common ground. We are the stuff that dreams are made of!

The Work

• List the things or situations which seem to create the most guilt for you. How would this be a good description of your shadow, that side of you which is the repository of what you have rejected and otherwise hidden away because it was somehow unacceptable, or guilt producing.

• Write up how you were punished as a child. What guilt, what fear, did this cause in you, and what were the attitudes towards yourself and life resulted from this? As an adult how do you deal or not deal with the consequences of your choices?

• Try meeting only your needs for a day. Consistently tell other people "no" and at the same time deal with the tension which this produces. What attitudes underlie the tension you are experiencing? Then try only meeting other people's needs for a day. What shifts in attitude and consciousness seem to result?

• Finally, practice balance in each situation. Always get a need met at the same time you are meeting someone else's need. If yours and the other person's needs cannot both be met, stay in the creative tension until you find a way through to something new.

Feel and you will not pass judgment.

§§§

Play

Image: *the tumbleweed blows across the prairie*

"To play the game of life is to not be identified with it."

We play when we act but do not identify with the action. Work is when we are identified with what we do.

The child plays at doctor, accident, war, house, making babies. The child copies the adults and rehearses the adult life by playing it out. The adult, on the other hand, takes Work as real by identifying with it, and to identify with anything is to be caught in it. To play the game of life is to not be identified with it. When we are not identified with what we do we have more flexibility and creativity available. If you do not like doing something, or cannot get into it because you cannot see yourself as it, then play with the energy, try it out as just a game.

Adults are identified with being adult. Children, on the other hand, are not as identified with being children. They play at all the roles of life. The adult gets lazy and picks a small number of roles and tries to identify with these, causing many deaths in the personality. To identify with one thing is to reject other things. "I am a good person," means "I am not a bad person." In actuality, being human we are both.

We can return to play, not competition, not winning and losing, but dancing into and out of an experience with a sense of discovery and endless possibility. We play to get out of our known selves. Branch out. Be everybody. To laugh is to recognize that we have over-identified with ourselves. To laugh and play, to express the child in us, is the renewal by which we are born anew each day.

The Work

• What would you do if you made an intention to play at least once a day?

• What are the three things in yourself or in life with which you are most identified? What causes you to be identified with them.

• What in terms of play might help you become free of your identifications?

• In what ways were you too serious as a child?

• In what ways did you let yourself play as a child? Why these areas and not others?

• What would be your own definition of play?

• Design a play program for yourself. Or take your main activities and add a play element to them.

Play kindles the flames of renewal and letting go.

§§§

The First Choice

Image: *a hidden waterfall under a mountain*

"At the end of that long train ride into my future I made
someone pay a little for my suffering."

My earliest memory of making a choice was at age six when I was sent off
to boarding school, never again to live in my parents' home. I can see it
now, the little boy dressed up with the name tag hung around his neck. My
mother is telling me about courage. My father is carrying my suitcase. In
my heart I don't know why this is happening. I cannot comprehend the
inevitable. Yet it is happening to me. I want to cry, but I am supposed to
be strong. I want to cling, but I am supposed to be independent. I want to
stay at home, but I am forced to take a journey.

I was placed on the train leaving New York City's Grand Central Station
and given the name of the town in upper New York state where I was to
get off and be met by the school staff. I was to listen for the conductor's
calling out each station as we came to it. The conductor was also to make
sure I got off at the right station. The conductor called out "Hope Farm". I
knew this was my destination, but in my child's mind I was not sure. I was
not absolutely certain that I had heard right. I wanted to do the right thing
so I waited. The train moved on again. I think I went to the conductor and
the school people had to drive to the next town and pick me up for my new
life.

It seemed I had no choice in the matter. I had to leave home at age six. I
just had to leave. That's all. Destiny was handing me an uncommon blow,
and what would I do with it?

What choices did I have? Perhaps even in this forced situation I still had
choice. There is always a measure of freedom given to us in any moment.

How well do we take and use that freedom?

At the end of that long train ride into my future I made someone pay a little for my suffering. But I also weakened my choice-making ability by my hesitation and insecurity. I could have gone with what I knew was right, that this was my station and that I had accept the change fully. If I got off at the wrong station and there was no one there to meet me, it would be like stepping off into the void. I would leave my new home, the train, and step out into nothingness. It was so hard at that moment to trust in the future and in strangers.

The early choices are the crucial, the mythic ones. To this day, I can become extremely anxious when faced with preparing for a trip. But the pattern is changing. Strong choice becomes the necessity and the cure. Choice is directing energy in one direction and not another. Automatic actions are not choices in this sense. To choose we must place ourselves within the tension of mutually exclusive alternatives. Saying Yes to one thing is saying No to all which would oppose it.

I was given destiny at an early age. I was awakened from childhood. I was given a rough choice. I was to bear the consequences of someone else's cruel choice. Yet within the context of it all I still had some freedom, and it is upon that which I evaluate my behavior. Perhaps, in staying on the train past my destination, I made the choice I was capable of. I could think of nothing else. It has taken years to work through the insecurity which has plagued my choice-making ability. And now I love my myth. For I was given in the black light of consciousness the power of choice. Nothing is certain in this world except our necessity to make choices.

The Work

• Was what happened to me in childhood fair in your estimation? What do you mean by fairness? How does justice relate to choice-making?

• What is your earliest or most significant childhood memory of choice-making on your part? Be specific and write about it. Let the feelings and imagery come up. Then analyze your choice-making, or lack of choice-making, pattern.

• Describe how you make choices. On what basis do you usually make choices? Feelings? Others' opinions? Intuition? Thinking rationally about the situation? Doing what is right according to your beliefs? Other?

What we choose is what we become.

§§§

Some Sayings for the Journey

We are already the goal of what we would become.

•

To journey is to go where you hesitate to go.

•

To journey is to know right where you are.

•

There is no going back. The return takes us to the end of all our days.

•

You will only know where you are going when you get there.

•

What we least expect is what happens to us.

•

Never look back or you will be blind to the future.

•

To journey is to match inner life to outer.

•

We spend the first half of life catching up, and the second half moving ahead.

•

Live the process and the goals will take care of themselves.

•

The goal of life is what you do now, not later.

•

There is no future, only your becoming in the now.

•

A riderless horse never seeks a master.

•

Moving towards sunset may bring the sunrise.

•

There is no return, only completion.

•

You are already on a journey. The task is to find what journey you are on.

The Journey

Image: *a wooden staff carved by The Maker*

"The great question is, are we fulfilling ourselves at the deepest of levels?"

"Once upon a time... and they lived happily ever after." Yes, but what is between the beginning and the end of every folk tale? The Journey.

"Once upon a time..." starts us out in eternal time back at the beginning of things, and is the prelude for our entering the Now of the story. And "...they lived happily ever after." takes us back into eternity. Life may be seen as a journey when we recognize that what we are going through has underlying universal patterns to realize the meaning of life. The archetypes are the primaries of existence and every journey contains those primaries within it. It is our fate to encounter crisis as Death-Rebirth, sexuality as the striving for unity in the Self, a continual movement forward in life as the Journey, sickness as the Adversary, prosperity and new life as the Heroic, caring as the Feminine, and structuring as the Masculine. Do we resist any of these archetypes? Then we resist the journey and seek refuge in unconsciousness.

How each of the primary elements play themselves out in each person's life will differ, even among twins. Perhaps in childhood you had a huge dose of the Adversary and needed to almost overdevelop its opposite, the Heroic? Or perhaps, in striving for the unity you did not have, you seek much sexual activity? Whatever the dynamics, we can make them conscious and create balance and resolution in our lives.

Each person has a destiny to realize in this life. The question is, are we fulfilling ourselves at the deepest of levels? To do this we must accept fully whatever comes our way, in sickness and in health, in good fortune and in bad, and in dealing with all the contraries which are our lot.

It all started back in childhood. What was the journey for us then? What did we resist and what did we accept? We return now to those experiences in childhood to make them conscious and integrate the totality of what happened to us. We see and re-experience the Journey as it carried us through childhood. The Journey continues into adult life and finally to the end of all our days.

The Work

• Construct a journey map of the first six years of childhood, including your roots going back before you were born. Include experiences related to the various topics we have been dealing with. To create a journey map you draw a winding road on successive sheets of paper linked together. Include intersections and other roads leading into and going away from it. You also label and draw little figures and scenes representing your primary experiences. Primaries might include you as journeyer, parents, other family members, crucial or strong events, traumas, gifts, spiritual experiences. The list is endless. You might make a cut-out of you as journeyer, and cut-outs for anyone or anything which goes with you. Don't forget your mythic experiences and figures.

• In what ways are you on and not on a journey? Have you committed yourself to following the path of greatest meaning in life? Or have you focused on worldly and collective goals and values as substitutes for the Journey? To journey is to move below the surface of things. We don't all make it.

• Write up your first six years and before as a folk tale using the traditional motifs. "Once upon a time so-and-so lived in a... etc., and had to deal with... etc., and was helped by... etc., and was almost overwhelmed by... etc., and finally got to... etc., and lived harmoniously until the next gate opened in her, or his, journey." There are other motifs and aspects of a typical folk tale, of course. Create what works for you. Perhaps read again your favorite folk tale and then go from there. Let it flow!

Life puts you on the road but how you walk it is your affair.

§§§

Which Sex Were Each Of Your Parents?

Image: *crossed sticks in the middle of the path*

"My father mothered me and my mother told me what to do. Am I confused?"

The great, well-kept secret is that our parents often changed "sexes" right before our eyes. No wonder we became confused and unclear about which role models to follow. Am I a boy, or am I not? Am I a girl or not?

One kind of mother problem can be defined as having grown up in conflict with ones mother's animus, her inner masculine. Did your mother act out of her feminine, her caring, accepting and nurturing side? Or was she critical, directing and dominating? One father problem can be having grown up in conflict with one's father's anima, his inner feminine. Was your father strong, definite and structuring? Or was he touchy, passive, and withdrawing? Perhaps some of these characteristics apply to your parental experience in those early years. Our thesis is that often the parent acts out the opposite archetype to the biological predisposition with confusing results.

If I as a boy am seeking nurturing and acceptance from my mother and instead get criticism and domination, I am missing what I feel I need. In this example, my mother is acting from her negative animus. Her animus is out to defeat and destroy my young masculine to keep me chained. And my father's masculine is not strong enough to balance my mother's masculine, so she rules the roost. If however, my mother is able to also act out of her feminine and be nurturing and inspiring, then my own masculine can grow and achieve in the world. I will not be in competition with my mother's animus and therefore free to develop.

In my life mother did rule the household. It was she who taught me about great literature and music, who discussed the great ideas and movements of this century while my father cooked the meals for us and took me to movies and to buy toy guns which I loved. My father was the well known poetry anthologist of the sixties, Oscar Williams, but he never once discussed a serious idea with me. Where was his masculine in relation to his son? I don't know.

Certainly, we each have the opposites within us, but when we express the opposite of our natural dominant in an unconscious and compulsive way we create a loaded atmosphere. How clear are you on your relation to the archetypes of the Feminine and Masculine? To find out, see how they operated in your parents, and your reactions to what was or was not being expressed. Then make choices to evoke healing energies for balance and integration.

My father mothered me and my mother told me what to do. Am I confused? At least I got something from them. No wonder I wondered who my real parents were!

The Work

• How did your father act as a mother, and your mother as a father? Or was there some other combination with them? What effect did this have on you?

• Did either of your parents want you to be a different sex than you came into the world with? If so, what effect has this had on you in terms of masculine and feminine?

• How, as a small child, did you evoke your parents' archetypal opposites?

• How did you become either a parent's "symbolic lover", intimate friend, or adversary? How does this pattern affect present intimate relationships?

What we lack outside can be fulfilled within.

§§§

The Wounded Child

Image: *the meteorite has fallen out of the sky*

"Experiencing our wounds can make us whole."

Who wants to go back into that painful past and experience the worst again? Who wants to experience one's own wounded child? Was she teased unmercifully or violated in some way? Was he punished arbitrarily for things he didn't understand? Did the child feel powerless and therefore act out in ways which would upset the parents? Breaking things? Getting into accidents and being hurt? Temper tantrums? Or did one have to be the good child all the time when it would have been so nice to fall apart and be taken care of? But who would have helped us if we had let go to our vulnerability?

Picture the modern scene. We are all clients in therapy with someone. Do we let go there? Do we show our most vulnerable side? Do we trust that the therapist will respond in an accepting and healing way? Perhaps we have tried to let go, to become vulnerable in our intimate, adult relation-ships, and the other person could not or would not handle this? If someone else cannot handle our vulnerable side, how can we?

Is it so bad to have a wounded child? We hurt. We cry out in pain. We want to avoid painful situations in the present life because they also evoke the unbearable repressed trauma of childhood. Yet we need to work through the wounded child in order to be able to fully deal with the pain natural to adult life. The solution is to let go to vulnerability with one part of oneself while maintaining support and balance with the ego and the Self, the integrative center. We can seek and receive help from others, but ultimately the bailout only goes so far, and we must face our own wounded child on our own terms and with our own resources.

It's all right to have a wounded child who breaks out every once in a while. Perhaps it happens in sickness or when we are denied something we think we need. Perhaps the woundedness comes through when we let go in other ways, such as in making love. Or does the wounded child make its presence felt in some nameless anxiety or consuming compulsion, such as greedy over-eating?

The principle is to know and safely express one's wounded child in ways which seem appropriate. Otherwise, this childishness will break out in inappropriate ways, giving us much trouble in order to get our attention. The wounded child is our vulnerability. Experiencing our wounds can make us whole. When we are most vulnerable we are most human, and therefore able to be cared for by ourselves and others. When we are vulnerable we are less arrogant, and therefore easier to approach and be intimate with on a human level. Our vulnerability makes us real.

The Work

• Describe your earliest experience of being wounded.

• How would you describe your wounded child? Write in free flowing words and images.

• Have a dialogue with your wounded child, how it affects your life right now, and what it wants from you? Then take action.

• What is an example of how your wounded child breaks out in adult life? What feelings or issues are usually behind its breaking out?

• Finish this sentence, I like being vulnerable because...

Relationship is shared vulnerability.

§§§

Childhood's Stories

Image: *her face has aged a hundred years*

"I do not know any babies who are fatalistic. I know many adults who are."

Rock-a-bye baby on the tree top.
When the wind blows the cradle will rock.
When the bough breaks the cradle will fall.
Down will come baby, cradle and all.

Now what kind of a song is this to sing to a baby? This lullaby gives an interesting yet pessimistic viewpoint on life. The fall from grace? The weakness of the support system? Be careful of high places? Do not reach for the sky, little one, or great will be your fall! Life is full of danger, my little one, my baby, and you may not make it. Do not set your sights too high. Expect the worst. And what is baby doing up in that tree in the first place? Is this an unconscious death wish by the parent to be freed of the child and young again? Where is the parent who will protect baby?

Jack and Jill went up the hill
To fetch a pail of water.
Jack fell down and broke his crown
And Jill came tumbling after.

Dear Jack and Jill,

I want you to know that water is one of the wonderful things in life, and I am glad that you are doing your part in going and getting some water for yourself and others. Sometimes we do take a tumble when we try and help ourselves or others. But much of the time we can walk happily down hills and not fall and break our crowns. And, Jill and Jack, if we can stop war and reduce the level of violence in this world things will go better for you and all of us. Life does not need to be an endless tragedy, and we do not have to feel so helpless when we seek to get our needs met. When you go up that hill to fetch your water, come back down to us also with love and caring in your buckets. Watch your step please. Together we may just make it into a new and better world. I love you. You are doing fine.

Jack and Jill came off the hill
With many pails of water.
Jack went down and into town
And Jill came sailing after.

Each one of us in childhood has been drawn to some folk tale or Mother Goose rhyme. Why a particular one? Looking closely at the tale or rhyme we can see mirrored there a certain view of the world which probably has colored how we see and interact with life as adults. For transformation sometimes we must go back to the beginning, to the early lore reflected in images before adult thinking. The archetypes, the primal energies, are most raw in childhood and in mental illness. In some ways Mother Goose may reflect a collective psychosis or archetypal possession from ancient times, and out of which we are, hopefully, slowly emerging.

I do not know any babies who are fatalistic. I know many adults who are. For transformation we return to the wondrous child before the wounded child showed its being.

Yes, there were also the miracle stories, the fairy godmother who saves Snow White and helps her out in the end. But I prefer that we not wait to the end of things for redemption. Wherever there is darkness and evil, there is also the possibility for its redemption. The child itself is its own redeemer. Redemption comes in the process of living life. Redemption, to have major effect, must come in the middle of a life story, not at the end.

The Work

• What story or rhyme out of childhood where you most drawn to? Look at it closely as you would a dream. How has its message influenced your life? Outline the major points of your childhood which seem mythic. Then put them into a Mother Goose rhyme or into folk tale form. What does this experience inspire in you?

As you believe, so shall you act.

§§§

The Companion

Image: *a pair of eyes gleam in the night*

"...we need others in order to find ourselves."

Life is a lonely business at times, and perhaps always. Ultimately, we are alone in this life. We make connections, some deep and lasting. Yet even before we are on our death bed, we know it, we sense that it's only us in the universe. There are some things we will never be able to share with anyone.

Hence the companion, that mythic journeyer who goes with us down the path of life and even to the edge of eternity. And who is my companion, ultimately? Who is it who understands and brings out that which is essentially me?

Shall I make you my companion this year? Are you the one with whom I can share? Are we soul-mates? Do we have a deep intunement without doing anything to make it happen?

In childhood, many of us had imaginary companions, "the elementals" as some people would call them. Perhaps they were most present when we were alone, and the adults knew nothing about them? But they talked to the child us, and made little magical things happen in our lives. They knew who we were and how we felt. We could tell them anything and they would understand. They had secret powers which they might loan to deal with the crazy life we found ourselves in. Perhaps we saw them as guides, ones who knew the future and made the right things happen, the ones who came to us in our time alone.

Then there was also the best friend, the real outer life friend with whom we did everything and said everything. Well, almost. Sometimes there would be disappointments, conflicts, fights, and we would feel all alone again. Perhaps we wanted our friend to be someone they weren't? But we needed that person to talk to, to with move through our day.

And so comes the point of integration, the realization that we need others in order to find ourselves. The secret of relationship becomes one of not holding on to the people we relate to, but rather integrating into ourselves the energy they carry and evoke for us. We learn that we use our closest intimates to find more of ourselves. I will be a mirror and a companion to you as we live our lives. But in the same way I rely on you to reflect me back to myself so that I may truly become the person I am meant to be. I seek to become a companion to myself, to all of you out there, to life, to my guides, and ultimately the Source which directs me and to which I return at the earthly end.

The Work

• Describe your imaginary companions in childhood, especially those first years. If you have no factual memory, then meditate and sink back into early childhood, and see yourself with an imaginary companion.

• How would you characterize your strongest childhood friendships? What needs were being met or not being met in these relationships?

• What are you seeking in companionship these days? What light might the thoughts expressed in the above passage throw on your companionship needs?

• What kind of companion are you to others? Evaluate. Where would you like to give more? Where are you giving too much?

• What function does your journal play in meeting your needs for companionship?

We relate to others to relate to ourselves.

§§§

Playing Victim

Image: *he looks at his hand while it burns*

"In the family some dominate and some play victim."

As a child I was terrorized, sexually abused, deprived, spit upon, rejected time and time again. Am I complaining? Do I hate my childhood? Not at all! I realize now that was just good training for playing the victim in life. I didn't go so far as to put my head in the way of a fist during a fight, as another boy did, but I had my tricks. There are two ways to win a fight. One is to overpower and victimize your opponent. The other is to make yourself into the perfect victim. I was never good at the latter, though I could whine and sulk on occasion. I learned to control my tears, to become cold and somewhat hard. I hated the weak, the vulnerable, the crazy, the morally decrepit. I would be the little hero no matter what. But I was a victim at heart.

Playing victim is sinking into despair and lack of intentionality when reality seems to be presenting me with things other than what I want. When reality becomes my adversary I can play victim by giving up, as if saying, "all right, if you don't want me to succeed, I won't."

"What does it matter if things don't go my way? We lose some, we win some. The law of opposites holds sway over our lives. The great archetypal figure of Fortuna, the medieval goddess of fortune who holds the balance scales, will have her way no matter what I choose."

Wait! These are attitudes. What a thing to tell oneself! Better to say that I am open to any opposite but my choice goes with that which is most unifying and integrating. I may not get what I want, but I will use whatever potentials are present in the situation for the best.

Playing victim is telling oneself that something bad is going to happen anyway, so why try? Playing hero is telling oneself that all is going to turn out to be wonderful, just the way one intends it to. Playing victim leads to despair. Playing hero leads to inflation. Surely there is an integrative way.

Playing victim is also a manipulation pattern established in early childhood to get our needs met. The formula is, if we are wounded and helpless someone will take care of us. In the family some dominate and some act the victim. The dominators project their wounded side onto natural victims, they are drawn both to helping and victimizing further. The victims project their strong side out onto natural dominators and so stay in dependency. To get free you must give up manipulating with helplessness and take on your own self-healing. Use others for support but more and more do your own work yourself. Wholeness means integrating both the wounded and the healing into one.

The journeyer is one who does not consciously slip into any one archetypal configuration, but who is fully present in the situation as it is. We do not deny either possibility but instead work with both to achieve the ultimate value, which is the presence of wholeness.

The Work

• The journeyer, in your own words, is one who…

• What is a recent example of your playing victim in adult life?

• List your victim attitudes. Then rewrite these attitudes into affirmations to change them. What are the significant results?

• Describe your victim complex as best you can. Check it out with people who know you. Then picture and describe an image of greater wholeness for yourself.

We do to ourselves what has been done to us.

§§§

God

Image: *the whirlwind hovers over a dry lake*

"What is the religion of childhood?"

In childhood I had a relationship with God which lasted for years. God came in where my parents failed me. Where they were effective I did not need God.

From the earliest years until around age thirteen I had a bed wetting problem. I could not control my bladder when I fell asleep. Today this is one of the things which has made the night so powerful for me. In the night things happened, not of my own choosing. In the night I would be decisively defeated time after time. In the night it was only me against my unknown antagonist, God. And it was in the night that I learned to pray year after year for rescue by a new God, a God who never answered my prayers.

Almost every evening for three years I prayed to God not to wet the bed and almost every night I wet the bed. My parents hated it and tried and tried to figure out what to do. One vivid time I was put down for a nap at their friend's house and I wet right into the couch. I would wake up at boarding school, and always too late, feeling the embarrassing clammy wetness. And I would stay awake for hours, rubbing dry sheet against wet, trying to get the sheet dry and the stains out so that no one would notice in the morning and I wouldn't be embarrassed once again.

There was no God in childhood for me. There was only a lonely, desperate boy's cry for help. Religion would have to be terribly real if this boy were later to accept it.

Many of us leave childhood either rejecting God as we reject the parents, or having been rejected by them. We feel rejected by God because we were not saved from the worst of childhood, and in the adult life ahead we see more evil and destructiveness ahead. Many times when we seek religion and God we are looking for the healing relationship we feel we never got in childhood. We project the ideal parent onto our G-O-D image which becomes then the ideal parent in the sky. Religions themselves try to be the ideal family to their followers. Their leaders are idealized and have the role of giving and receiving love.

The first lesson of transforming childhood is to accept reality exactly as it is. To project parental longings onto a G-O-D image and onto a religious community and its leaders is common and unwise. It takes us away from accepting life as it is and doing self-integration as our life task.

G-O-D may in fact exist as the prime mover of the universe and as a guiding force in our lives. But how will we ever find and relate to this Centrality if we are still in a state of projection onto deity because we have not solved our childhood problems?

The Work

• What is your earliest experience of God? Or what was your earliest or main spiritual experience in childhood? Write about it and its significance.

• How do you react to the above passage about this child's longing to be saved from wetting the bed? Why was he not saved?

• What is your present position regarding God and spiritual experience?

• What was your early childhood experience of your parents as God? Did they fail you or influence you in terms of your own spiritual experience? What is the child's general experience of God? Write a description of God from a child's point of view?

The presence of G-O-D is in the absence.

§§§

The Divine Child

Image: *the earth opens to reveal a new spring of water*

"...the Great Gift, is the Divine Child,..."

And the angel of the Lord came upon them and said, "Behold, this day is born to you a savior who is Christ the Lord." Within the Christian religion there are many beautiful Christmas hymns all focused on worshiping a Baby, a Divine Child.

What is this new birth, and why does it happen in the dead of winter? At the darkest time of the year many ancient religions celebrated the birth of a savior, a divine child. It is also the time of miracles and light, as in the Jewish holiday of Hanukkah, the festival of lights.

Christmas as a cultural holiday has lasted centuries because it is based on a constellation of archetypes. Christmas comes around the time of the winter solstice, the darkest time of the year when the new light is born. A divine baby is an appropriate symbol for this event since it is the natural consequence of a union of opposites, the masculine and feminine. The holiday itself is an intersection of the archetypes of Death-Rebirth and the Journey, of cyclic time and historical, linear time.

The family archetype is especially prominent at this time with many people returning to their original families and stuffing themselves, trying to fill up again with parental sustenance to last a full year. Those not in a fulfilling relationship can become depressed. They may feel excluded from the family circle and the celebration of new life. If you cannot look forward to new life you are going to feel badly at a time when it is being most celebrated.

Your whole traumatic and needy childhood may become evoked at Christmas and consequently you may feel depressed. Or you may feel like rushing around trying to preserve the family archetype by buying presents for everyone. Childhood was a needy time, a time in which you needed to be given to constantly. So in adult life each Winter Solstice millions of people go scurrying around trying to buy just the right present, attempting with gifts to fulfill needs never met in childhood. Watch your gift giving. How much of it is buying what you yourself want? You may have been taught to buy parental love by being good and now at Season's Greetings you again try to buy with gifts other people's love.

The only gift, the Great Gift, is the Divine Child, the possibility of new birth in the coming year, a birth which is at once unifying and personal to you and also new hope and growth for your culture and for the world.

The Work

• What were your earlies winter celebrations like?

• What are your feelings and attitudes about giving gifts? What are you honestly doing? What would be a constructive inner attitude to follow in giving?

• How can you help the Divine Child be alive in you this year? This is meant as an archetype, not a religious figure. It does not have to be symbolized as it is in Christianity. If you paint the symbol, let it come naturally to you.

• What comes up for you in the Winter Solstice transition regarding the family archetype? How might you deal with these things? How has your family's celebration of the Winter Solstice influenced your life?

Celebration is the heart's acceptance of healing and grace.

§§§

The Christian Mandala

The Christian mandala occurs at the Winter Solstice, the darkest time of the year, the time of gestation and loss of light. A healing mandala is particularly needed at this time. Note that in our diagram we also include other primary religious symbols such as the snake of the Garden of Eden and Herod, the wicked king who tries to murder the Christ child. Traditional Christianity does not include Herod in the Cresch scene because it has a strong bias towards excluding rather than including evil as part of the total religious process. Since we are Jungian and use a wholeness perspective, we include the darkness very much present at the time of the birth of light.

The Christian Mandala As Represented In the Birth Story Circa 300 AD

A Six Year Old

Image: *a child looks out the window*

"…this my spirit you must keep."

Who is this darling six year old who loves to play with me, ride piggy-back on my shoulders, and cries so easily if I am too rough with him? Such energy, such happiness, and such tears. My heart suffers with you when you fall off the slide and hurt yourself. You cannot control the reality or your body and painful things are happening to you. I cannot prevent some of these things.

You are a warm child, a bright child, full of the fun of life and always asking for things. Such energy keeps me moving and sometimes I cannot stand it anymore, and I have to say No to you. You decide what you will and will not eat. I coax and command you but your will seems superior to my own. If I am to have my way, I will have to put out more energy than you and pay the consequences of your displeasure. You are not easy to defeat, even in your own interest, and I love you.

At night I put you to bed, tell you a story, sing you a song, and say with you a prayer I wrote.

> O God, as I go to sleep,
> this my spirit you must keep.
> Send a guardian angel from on high
> and give a dream as I lie.

I have modified the traditional image of childhood. I have made it not so dark for you and me. It no longer is, as in the traditional prayer, "If I die before I wake, I pray the Lord my soul to take." For you see, I want you to stay right here on earth. I do not want to lose you. You are my child. You are my hope. You are my inner delight and sadness, my creativity and vulnerability, my play and my spontaneity, my hope for the future and my lost past. I need you to be alive in me.

The Work

• How do you respond to this description? What does it evoke for you?

• Why not write a description of a six year old as it comes to you? You do not have to have an actual experience of a six year old. Think of yourself as a six year old, or just let your imagination take it where it will.

• What happened to you around age six? Perhaps there was some major transition or event? What was the essence, the "life point" then?

• What is one way you sometimes act like a six year old now?

• Are you happy? Why? Why not? Are you defining happiness in terms of your childhood, or in terms of your more mature, adult years?

We go to the child to find the adult.

§§§

Your Earliest Childhood Dream

Image: *a fire burns the landscape*

"That earliest dream may be in a sense our destiny,"

We remember from childhood what is of central importance to our personality. Within the psyche reside the patterns created in childhood. Let us then go to the dream, that reflection of the trembling myth in the inner world.

We went to our bed one night and had a great dream, a dream of major proportions which probably scared us awake.It was of such great intensity that we remember it still. This dream may have repeated itself in one form or another throughout our childhood. Perhaps its symbols and themes still come into our dreams in adult life.

What is possible is that the remembered dream from childhood is one which reflects our personal myth, a basic pattern which we have been living out all our lives. Was it that tiger trying to get into the room with two doors? We would go to one door and hold it closed, and the tiger would go to the other door and try to enter to devour us. In adult life such a dream would reflect a constant fear of invasion, and insufficient ability to cope with life's stresses. To find healing the dreamer can reenter the dream as an adult and help that little child deal with the tiger. What are the alternatives? Leave the situation and try to find a room with only one door? Go out of the room and face the tiger down and see what it wants? Let the tiger in and make friends with it, and use its power for new life? Let the tiger in and let oneself be devoured in the dream state and see what happens next?

First we look at the basic pattern reflected in the dream. In this example life is seen as scary and dangerous, and the dreamer's reaction to this fear is to engage in defensive action rather than change a fundamental attitude that powerful things will destroy me. Then we must reflect on how the dream has been lived out in one's outer life. With this dreamer her anger and relations with men were often overpowering for her.

By working with the dream, we can change defeating patterns and attitudes to more effective and healing ones. That earliest dream may be in a sense our destiny, our problem to solve before we can be free to fulfill ourselves in adult life.

Every life situation is in fact a double bind situation. Any energy can in effect go either way in life and often choices make all the difference. As in the dream, you may not be able to keep the tiger out, but you can sometimes choose by which door he or she is to enter.

The Work

• Write up your earliest childhood dream, first the basics you remember and then an elaboration or fuller imaginative description of it.

• What does your childhood dream say about yourself as a child? What is the pattern there? Is it resolved, brought to completion or is resolution still needed? How has the pattern in the dream been acted out throughout your life?

• Do a dream re-entry with your eyes closed. See the dream again and experience it, but this time bring in the "adult you" and help the "child you" out so that new feelings and imagery appear in order to bring completion. If this is hard or fearful for you, ask someone skilled to guide you through the dream. Or rewrite the dream, bringing it to resolution. What is significant about the resolution which comes? Elaborate, then write down some commitments for change in your life based on changes in the dream.

We are the dream dreaming us.

§§§

Death In The Family

Image: *a gate blowing in the wind*

"If you can face death you can face life."

Death... Death in the family. It may have been only a little one, or it may have been very close to you. Your father or your mother, your brother or your sister. Possibly a grandparent or some other relative. Perhaps you did not know death directly this early in childhood. Yet somehow death entered your consciousness and evoked in you the ultimate questions.

Do all things die?

Is so-and-so gone forever?

Where do things go when they put them in the ground?

Possibly these questions came to you more from the little things. The dead beetle in the back yard. Your pet dog that died a natural death, or was run over by a car. This recognition of absence, of mortality, is one of the births for the ego. The slim small ego of the child recognizes that someday it will be no more. There is at this age a certain clarity about one's place in the universe which often becomes muddled in the adult years with neurosis, egocentrism, identification with the world, and scientific and religious doctrines about reality.

Maybe it was a few years later than age six, but when did this question of death hit you and how did you survive it? Are you still afraid of death? Reentering your childhood experience of death, like you would reenter a dream, can help you come to terms with death. In death there may be new life, but there is no return to the old.

In childhood death seems far away, almost absent. Therefore many of us remain identified with being a child. We don't want the years to come in at us, chopping away at our substance, and finally taking us in the end. But perhaps we are not ready to die because we have not yet lived. We grew up too soon, and now as adults we pursue the lost childhood, hoping to avoid death until it has found us.

Some of us were taught by adults to avoid death. There was a death in the family and someone in authority decided that the little children should not be there at the funeral service. Nobody talked to us, people hid things from our ears.

Death for most adults is not the mystery it is for the natural child. If you can face death you can face life. For in each moment resides the choice to live or die. How we choose in the little things makes all the difference. In order to live we must die. We must sacrifice the old values, the worn-out ways of doing things, in order to practice a new potential. Life is the goal of life and dying the process.   Why not become that child again who wakes to each new day having let go of the old?

The Work

• Describe your early fundamental experience of death. Even if it was of someone very close to you, tell yourself about it once again, and in a way that sees death as natural and necessary to life. Not death, the great deprivation, but death, the teacher of my destiny. What has this childhood death experience to teach me?

• What is your present view of death? In what ways might it be influenced by early childhood experience?

• What, if any, connections between God and death did you make in childhood?

• We do not fear death if we have found life. Write your response to this statement. Write with flow and feeling!

Death gives life to life as life gives life to death.

§§§

The Soul

Image: *into the pool a stone drops*

"Does individuality survive death?"

Far away, even millions of light years away, abide the endless configurations of souls, the essences of those who have come and gone. Or do they still reside surrounding us, layer upon concentric layer, as near infinite sparks of being which once were in the flesh?

Does individuality survive death?

We may not know how to respond to that question. And yet throughout our lives many of us know transcendence. We experienc mysterious and strange things, things far greater than ourselves. In this sense the child knows more than the adult. For the child is soul, that essence which has not yet been fully accepted and merged into concrete life.

The soul is the spark of the eternal, the relation between a person and the Source. The Source transcends life yet gives life meaning. The soul is that which transcends death, yet, unless we have worked to have our souls transcend life, the spark will be pitiful indeed.

There is no bank in heaven. You spend now and learn what you are doing. You can develop an enduring perspective outside yourself. The soul is what detaches us from life.

Return to childhood. Return to childhood now, the first phase of experiencing soul. Perhaps you knew it all before you arrived. Your soul, your unique essence, may or may not have wanted to be born in the flesh.

Suddenly you found yourself alive and in a body. And you spent many years thus limited and excited by life. And still you had those transcendent experiences, those chorales of eternity, of deep knowing, that you would struggle a life-time to put into words. You would elude your soul but it would not elude you.

Somehow you could not be completely who the others thought you were. You had experiences, you knew that there was more to life than "they" seemed to be conveying to you. You were a stranger in their midst and they were trying to reach for you, to make you one of them.

The soul knows no boundaries. Prepare! Let go, let go a long ways. When the birth is all over you will have begun.

The Work

• Are, you one of those who eagerly embraced coming into a body and being born? Are you one who loves life and wants to be here? Or do you feel yourself to be one of the reluctant ones who came to planet earth but never quite fit in? Does the world seem limiting? Do you long for much more than what seems to have fallen to your lot? Did you want entry into your body or do you feel it more as a forced choice upon you? What do you suppose explains your reluctance? How are you dealing with it now? What progress have you made in making your compromise with reality?

• What are you doing now at a daily levelto develop your soul, the eternal and essential part of yourself? What sacrifices are perhaps necessary to free your soul from too much worldly life? Do you feel there is a World Soul, a powerful entity which wants your soul to bond with it?

In the silences we are most real.

§§§

The Collective

Image: *the king sits on his old throne*

"The collective is all those rules, values and attitudes by which the group lives."

When I wake up in the morning, whose person am I? I was born into this world and immediately it laid its claim on me. The world wanted me for its own, and all too often I acquiesced. What was I to do? I had my needs and the world would meet my needs if I conformed to its expectations. For security I often gave up my individual self. For security I paid a price of conforming to the image of what a nice baby was to them.

I acted like them, so they thought I was one of them, and then met my needs. What was I to do? I was only a baby who had to have help to grow up in this world. Fairly soon I began to see the world as they did, to do the things they thought important. .

I had lost almost all sense of myself when they failed to meet my needs. The suffering they caused me made me realize that I was still an individual after all. I could not totally merge with the state, the religion, the group, the family. I was one individual in the world. I would have to figure out how to meet more of my own needs and try to understand this collective of which I was a part.

The collective is all those rules, values and attitudes by which the group lives. It is also the view of reality held by a culture and its people. On the inner plane, the collective is the attitudes and values from parents and society introjected within us, as well as the archetype of the group.

To rebel against the collective may be a necessary stage, but one nevertheless that is still very much tied to the collective, if only in reaction to it.

Rebellion creates the edge, the new emphasis in society for tomorrow. One generation rebels against the former by living out in a new way the shadow of the previous generation. We go from long hair to short hair, fromto looseness of attitude to highly structured attitudes, and so on. Each shadow lives out itself and creates a new shadow for the next generation to rebel against. This helps progress if it does not become an endless swinging back and forth.

To individuate we must disidentify from either merger or rebellion against the collective. We make peace with the collective, making conscious its values and world view, and working within it to achieve our own productivity and wholeness. Rebellion does not create a new identity, it creates an individual at war with the world and him or herself. The true individual is formed out of a unity of all the parts within and without.

In the same way, we must neither stay identified with inner dynamics nor flee from them by focusing strictly on the outer world. To individuate, we work to integrate both inner and outer.

At some point, because we are not identified with it, we emerge from the group a leader. People see in us a special quality. We have free energy for living at the edge of new possibilities.

We can be sacrificed by the collective or become the focus for its deepest aspirations and next development.

The Work

• What figure in history represents most for you what individuation is? What qualities especially appeal to you? How might these also be in you?

• What has been your history in relating to the collective? Merger? Rebellion? Other? What is your present relation to your own inner collective, your unconscious? In what ways are you willing to be an individual in this life?

What we leave unconscious rules us.

§§§

Processing The Void

Image: *hanging by one hand, nothing below*

"What we most fear will happen anyway."

You may feel you have not been exposed to it, but certain children do experience sometimes what feels like the loss of reality. Maybe you have woken up from a nap and find that you cannot move your body. Or one night you experienced indescribable terror. The walls move... the floor gives way... the ceiling is falling in. What started as a bad dream seems to breaks through into waking life also. These occurrences remind us that beyond our known limits of reality rests the void. All our activities and immersion in the everyday world keep back the utter darkness. But when the known images of who we are, of who we identify as ourselves, dissolve, we encounter the swirling void of lostness. We literally do not know who we are or where there is firm ground on which to stand.

As children we resist the void. We try to flee from it into our mother's arms, into soft, warm, human flesh. We hide from it in our fantasies of hero and heroine. We do little rituals to keep back the face of the deep. As adults our worlds may fall apart from time to time, and again we experience the void.

Part of transforming our myth of childhood is to process the void. If we know how, we can process the void by plunging into it. Fleeing from the void into the known will not help us with our ultimate fears. Facing the nothingness behind the surface of concrete and emotional reality will give us the strength to take on almost anything in life.

And why not face the void? What we most fear will happen anyway. Each of us through the great gateway of death will enter the void. The more we learn to face the empty darkness while still alive, the more we will savor and live the fullness of life. Facing the darkness is the ultimate task for anyone who would master fate.

The Work

• What was your most terrifying childhood experience of utter nothingness? Describe in detail so that your pattern for dealing with darkness can become somewhat clear.

• What today is your experience of ultimate darkness? How does it relate to your childhood experience?

• Reexperience, if you can, a childhood experience of the void, but this time bring the adult you into the situation to help your inner child feel secure in dealing with the experience. Do not save the child. Support it in confronting the void.

• Reexperience your most recent encounter with the void, one in which you were not in control and felt no known boundaries or resources at your disposal. This time do not resist it in any way, but go through it to strengthen your ego. Make sure you have competent support available in case you become overwhelmed.

• Do a meditation on the void, contemplate it and see what moves in you. In contemplating the void, process any fears that come up. Behind all your relative fears is probably one great fear. Experience this directly and go through it. What gets evoked? What becomes resolved?

• Paint the void in an imaginative way.

Experiencing the void cleanses us of our unreality.

§§§

Peers

Image: *five apples and a pear have fallen from the same tree*

"I had to fit in, for I felt my life depended on it."

My example is unusual but vivid. Strange as it may seem, at home I was not allowed to play with other children my age in those earliest years of my childhood. Then at age six I was sent away to boarding school, never to return home again, except for short yearly vacations. There I had to fit in, for I felt my life depended on it. There was always the group bully, like the little Italian kid, I feared and appeased. There were also those who liked me and with whom I could form friendships. In those early years I was never the leader when we played games of war and hide-go-seek. I did not feel liked enough to be a leader, but I made an excellent assistant to the leader. I would run errands fast, and make good suggestions for strategy.

Things changed when I was sent to military school at age twelve. There leadership was only partly based on outgoing friendliness. The military had hundreds of obvious standards to be measured by. I made good grades, trained well at military drill, and worked hard. I received promotions, class presidencies, and respect in certain quarters. I also made enemies, all those who were my competitors for the rewards. I learned to fear how the group mood could change and pounce on each one of us in turn.

The times when I was alone, or with only one other friend I could trust, were the best times, the most secure. The outer collective seemed too powerful and fickle to trust. In my late teens and twenties I became a rebel and feared the collective even more. My peers were both hell and heaven on earth. We both hated each other and soothed each other's wounds. We had fun, we played, and dreamed of a world we would someday control.

My heart goes out to my brothers and sisters everywhere. We are on a rocky boat together. We must cooperate with the collective. Our peers are a part of us, united we can change the world.

The Work

• You are in the early ages of childhood, say the period of six, seven and eight years old. You already have an idea of what the parents and society want. But you are spending most of your time doing your own thing with little people your age. What is it they want? What are the power dynamics within the group? What are their values? How have you suffered by not knowing how to fit into your group? Yes, you will go to parents and teachers for help, but they cannot be there to guard you all the time. You must seek allies within your own society. You are the next generation. Write about this experience as it happened to you.

• What kind of persona, or outer image of who you are, did you construct to get along with your peers? How did this change over the years?

• These days, what is your relation to a group? Your fears? How do you cope with groups? Why do you need groups?

• How do you get along with people of either sex your own age? What does this tend to say about yourself?

No boat is safe on a tumultuous sea.

§§§

The Road Not Taken

Image: *travelers resting at a wayside inn*

"In life, there are always at least two roads we travel."

T. S. Eliot gives a wonderful metaphor in a poem. He describes a magical garden somewhere which we can visit, where resides all the choices and paths contemplated but not taken. What then do we do with the unlived life? What would I be like today if only childhood had been different?

Return to childhood? What unlived life is still back there waiting to be born? If only my mother had not died or disappeared at age six or my father had not left when I was eight? Or if only I had had a sister or a brother, or not had a sister or brother? What is your magical childhood like?

In life, there are always at least two roads we travel. The outer one of actual accomplishment in physical reality, and the imaginary-archetypal one of inner reality. If we were condemned to live life only in the outer, where would we be? Most of us deny that the inner world is as real as the outer, and so we neglect it, not realizing that often experiences of archetypal reality have as much or more meaning as those which occur in the outer.

Scratch an adult and you get a child, a human being who is living out a magical kingdom of "what should have been" while dealing on the outside with the affairs of the world. Let us acknowledge the inner kingdom of fantasy for what it is and then let it go. Our goal, our health, is to live in the "here and now," not in a "reality" we would have liked. Yet take the magic, the fantasy, and honor it in thought and feeling by doing inner work around it which might actually lead to outer expression. You cannot live childhood over again, but you can redeem the past by acting differently in the present.

The Work

• What are some of the roads not taken for you? Explore and describe.

• Ideally, how would you have liked those early years to have been? Describe in detail and let your feelings come up.

• Explore and even write down your current fantasies. How might they be replicating childhood fantasies? What unlived life resides in those fantasies? What is the essence, the necessity, which you need to express more in present life? Look to your fantasies to signal needed life expression.

• See to what extent your present fantasizing is keeping you from being fully in the moment in present life. How can you enliven your present life with the energy behind your fantasies?

• How free are you from identification with outer reality? What percent of your day do you spend on inner matters? What changes are needed to strike a balance?

• Paint a picture, or a symbolic map, of childhood as you would have liked it to have been.

The life we live redeems the unlived life.

§§§

The Secret Sin

Image: *a bear stalks the outer meadow*

"True confession brings resolution, not absolution."

Each of us is hiding something from the world. Is it time to reveal that secret now? Is there anything about yourself which you have told no one in your life? Is it actually so terrible that it cannot be revealed?

Let us begin with the secret life of the child. There were so many prohibitions that we just had to break a few of them. Or were we one of those who never let ourselves get out of hand even in little things for fear we would be caught?

The secret of keeping a secret is that secrets preserve a certain image. If what I have done is unacceptable to others, it is likely to be unacceptable to myself. I confess my sins to accept them myself. True confession brings resolution, not absolution. We remain responsible to ourselves for what we have done. It does not go away into the chalice of forgiveness. It becomes more a part of ourselves. It loosens us up from an over-positive image we may have of ourselves. The great secret is the shadow, the seamy part of our personalities which gets acted out against our better judgment.

The more identified we are with our personas, the bright image of ourselves, the more compulsive becomes that which we reject about ourselves. To confess and mean it is to accept the shadow, not to give it away. Where will the shadow go if we do not take it in?

We have to hide sins for fear of the collective. If we were found out it would not go well with us. Yet we must create our sins to disidentify from the collective. What others consider sin may be what we need for integration.

And in adult years what would we like to keep hidden? The story of the shadow and its intrigues continue. What is one person's value is another person's sin. Elusive as the secret is, we must find it and reveal it to ourselves. Sometimes this means revealing it to others as well.

From the point of view of individuation, we are not so much interested in the acts of sin as we are in what lies behind them. What need, what archetype, is so corsing through our soul that it must seek expression in what is forbidden?

The Work

• List your darkest secrets from childhood, even the ones which you have told no one. What archetypal and personal energy might be behind them?

• If you do not seem to have much in the way of childhood sins, then list some close encounters where you wish that you had gone against the collective's values.

• List acts which make you doubt yourself or feel bad? In what ways do you feel the need to act against your own values or those of the collective?

• Is any sin unredeemable? What is redemption psychologically and spiritually?

To sin is to honor life with our imperfection!

§§§

Money

Image: *the sapphire in the light of the moon has brought the night closer*

"Money is a fiction. We are the reality."

Money is many things to many people, but what is it to us? In adult life most of us have never dealt with our psychological and spiritual attitudes towards money. Money is as much a psychological fact as it is a physical reality. One way to be free in the money sphere is to become free psychologically. Money is not only money, it is an attitude. Money is a piece of paper we and the collective believe in. In itself money floats away and burns like any piece of paper.

Back in childhood what did you hear and learn about money? Many of us were taught to use money as a way to measure self-esteem. We learned that the degree of prosperity we achieve is often related to the extent to which we believe in ourselves.

Money is not honest. It does not respond and reward us if we are good. Money does not give us a good time if we have lots of it, nor does it create happiness.

Money does not make us sick or deprive us. It is not what makes life hard for us. Money does not prepare us for death or give us the right friends. Money is one measure of our perception of reality, but it is not the value for which life has been created.

Money does not complain or sulk when we get mad. Nor does it heal us when we are sick. Money is power without choice, and what we choose to do with money reflects the values by which we live. Money is the medium, it is only one of the forms of energy exchange.

The key to prosperity is doing what is necessary to conserve our resources for both the up and the down times. For there will surely be dry periods as well as full periods in this existence. Another key is to keep a positive attitude towards developing the potential that is actually there in life. The third principle is to find and do what is in tune with our true nature and the world around us.

The core reality is what we must find for ourselves if we are to manifest the prosperity which is ours to give and receive.

The Work

• What were your earliest experiences of money? What attitudes were created for you around these experiences?

• What were each of your parent's attitudes towards money? How have these attitudes been acted out by you in your own life? What psychological and spiritual dynamics and principles might have been behind these parental attitudes?

• What of the above statements in the text did you respond to? What were your inner voices saying to you as you read the passage?

• Read the passage to a friend, or even a parent, and get their reaction. Use it as a basis for discussion and consciousness raising.

• What is the chief point, as you understand it, of our approach to money in this lesson?

• What is the most creative and dynamic position you can take personally towards money in your life? What will you do to manifest this position?

Money is reality but reality is more than money.

§§§

Dependency

Image: *the umbilical cord is wrapped around the baby's neck*

"Dependency is the shadow side of seeking fulfillment."

We all know the scourge of dependency in adult life. We depend on someone and then they fail us. We feel betrayed and hurt and may even vow not to depend on anyone ever again. Should there even be dependency in adult life? Or is this another one of those left-overs issues from childhood?

Real dependency is necessary. There are times when I might as an adult need to seek financial or medical help. There are also times when I might need to seek relational or therapeutic help.

Feigned dependency has some hidden motive • I am dependent when I expect you to do something for me • I am dependent when I am unable to do something for myself • I am dependent when I believe you will meet a need of mine because you said you would • I am dependent when I want you to contribute in some way to my welfare • I am dependent when I expect things for which I have not worked, or have not intended •

On the other hand, do I let go of my control whenever I seek help? Do I let myself be nurtured and supported? Some of us feel no one can do the job as well as we can. So we do not ask others to do anything for us because they might not meet our standards. This attitude can create its own form of dependency since we deny to ourselves the help that is naturally there from others and the universe. We over-depend on ourselves.

In neurotic dependency we manipulate or demand that our needs be met by others. The worst dependency is that of identification with the victim archetype. This is the hardest to self-cure because victim types believe that their wounds are greater than their ability to cure them. They manipulate others to see themselves as victims needing help. The piece missing in this puzzle is back in childhood. The child was in fact helpless and had to play helpless to get at least some of its needs met.

It would have been better for me and for everyone else who has had to deal with me, if more of my needs had been met. But they were not met and that is reality. No one has to meet my needs in this life. And what is more, no one will meet my needs just because I have them. People are concerned with their own needs. We meet our needs ourselves by tapping into healing places through our own choices and consciousness.

The dependency problem in adulthood is apparent when we hang around other people still demanding like a child to have our needs met. If this is an abundant universe, then go out and fulfill yourself. When you have a need only someone else can meet, present your need as a gift to them so that they will themselves be meeting a need of their own. And pay back your debts by learning to give to yourself what others first had to give to you.

Do not depend on others. Do not depend on yourself alone. In place of dependency put mutual creation. Your parents never met your needs fully, did they? And you survived? What was the secret?

The Work

• List some areas in your present life in which you feel compulsively dependent on someone or on a particular situation. What is your earliest recollection of being thus dependent? What shifts can you make?

• List some ways you feel too independent in adult life, in the sense that you will not let anyone help you or partake with you in the activity? What insecurity or attitudes might be behind this?

We are dependable when we are not dependent.

§§§

My Favorite Teacher

Image: *the wren brings worms to its nestlings*

"Without this one, this significant other, what would I be today?"

An old but vivid memory is taking me back many years. Miss Day was a communist, or so my parents told me years later. This meant that although it was all right to be a communist during the Second World War, she was later fired from her job as third-grade teacher of my boarding school.

The school was such a cold place to live, mainly because no one cared about me. I was just one of hundreds of children. Although they may have cared about all of us together, they could not take a warm interest in each one of us. But Miss Day cared for me. I felt that from the first. After the horrors of the night and dormitory life I would go off to school and there find acceptance.

Miss Day appears to me now as a bright sun, a warm sun on a cloudy planet. Learning is always a challenge for me, and she must have offered me warmth and acceptance for the mistakes I made, as well as praise for my accomplishments.

The significance for me is that somewhere in the crowd of all those people who were entrusted with my growth and upbringing one cared for me as a person. Without this one, this significant other, what would I be today? I could not have her as my mother, but her genuineness as a person gave me hope in enduring those dark years of childhood until I could be myself an adult.

The message I got from Miss Day is that there were warm people in the world capable of love, and that if I would make it through childhood, I would find them when I had the power to guide my own life.

And find them I did. Abundantly!

The Work

• What feelings and memories have come up for you now regarding a significant person early in your life? What is their meaning, their healing?

• Who was your favorite teacher in childhood, and why? Describe.

• What aspects of the parental archetypes might your favorite teachers have filled out for you?

• What also did the terrible teachers contribute to your life?

• Which is easier for you, to learn from books or to have someone else convey the information personally to you? What basis in your own childhood experience might your predisposition have come from?

What we need to learn in life will be taught to us one way or another.

§§§

School

Image: *a red and white ball tossed high in the air*

"What we most learned, or did not learn, in school is how to learn."

What feelings does the word "school" bring up for you? I feel "school" as an anxious challenge, a situation in which constant demands are put on me to control my behavior and learn, learn, learn.

What we most learned, or did not learn, in school is how to learn. What are my attitudes in adult life towards learning new things? What image do I have of myself as a competent learner? This is determined for better and for worse by my early learning experiences.

One incident comes to mind which has colored my whole life. I was having difficulty learning how to spell. I would be sent out of class with two girls to learn the assignment for the day. I didn't like girls at that age, and I learned to hate spelling. Getting a word wrong was considered the end of the world for me, a lack of perfection. It meant being laughed at and made to feel inferior, getting singled out in the group, being made to do extra work until I got the words right. My anxiety was always at a high level. I was in no way relaxed, and this made memorizing difficult.

Today, as an adult I do not spell well. But I have a love of words, and I am much more accepting of my own imperfection. I can laugh when someone points out a spelling error on my part. I have still created something real, even if it is misspelled.

And I do work to improve my spelling, trying to figure out why a word is spelled one way and not another. It is not the word I misspell, but the real anxiety about life which gets expressed, so I deal with that. It has become almost fun to redeem my childhood a little more with each new word I learn to spell with confidence and not anxiety.

The key experience in adult life which comes directly from our early learning is The Test, and the great anxiety this seems to produce in most of us. Typically we wake with a dream of not being prepared for an examination, or on stage and we have forgotten our lines. This reflects an archetypal situation in which we are challenged by a life opportunity or situation and dissolve in fear because we feel we lack the necessary information and resources to meet the challenge effectively. In school we studied for the exam, but not enough, and we almost failed. Daily in this life we are under challenge to meet the next crisis or opportunity and to deal with it successfully. Until we learn how to effectively meet challenge we will miss out on many of the most important things of life. The lesson from school is not the lesson. It is life. To be successful you must overcome your anxiety in any situation and use the resources available to bring resolution. Do not hesitate for long or life will pass you by. Better to fail than not to participate at all. But to succeed has the sweetest joy. If you did not get this in school, learn it now by learning the art of effectiveness.

To be effective we must open ourselves to a situation just as it is. Accept the situation, see its difficulties and opportunities, then choose that which has the greatest potential for resolution and new life. Do not hesitate. Make the decisive choices. Sacrifice all which stands in the way of the new choice, deal with the outcomes, and never look back.

The Work

• What are the major issues, attitudes, and self-images you picked up from school?

• Take one area or issue from your school experience and write about it. Describe your experience and the images, feelings, and attitudes it created in you. What, if any, have been the transformations in adult life?

• How would you describe your present learning pattern? Is it effective? Has it been cleansed of negative conditioning left over from childhood? What needs further work?

Living to learn must be balanced by learning to live.

§§§

The Great Betrayal!

Image: *the well is full of water but the pump is broken*

"Innocence is the prerogative of the child and the danger of the adult."

Somewhere in the passages of time we were trounced upon, even devastated. We were betrayed. Our faith in another person or in the world was destroyed, and thank God it was! Reality is a good cure for prolonged innocence. Innocence is the prerogative of the child and the danger of the adult.

"But you said you would."

"It's not fair."

"I trusted you!"

"I assumed you were going to do it."

"People should be nice to each other."

"Nobody lets me down and gets away with it."

Have you ever said any of these statements? Do you still say some of them, or other statements like them?

Everyone has felt more or less betrayed in childhood. Yet there can be no betrayal unless there is innocence. "Yes, they hurt me and it wasn't fair," you say. Of course it wasn't fair. And whoever said the world was fair? Your parents? You? God? Where did you ever get the idea that this was a just world with principles of right and wrong which people followed?

As a child you expected the world to be fair and just. You felt betrayed when you experienced unfairness, and wanted things to be different. The point is that these things were not different even though you didn't deserve them.

You had a very hard time accepting that you were the recipient of injustice and imperfection, and your young inner child has probably not gotten over it yet.

Perhaps you were fair and could be trusted. But be honest, if you were being the most good, weren't you manipulating your situation a little by being well thought of so as to avoid the heat of deprivation which might come your way?

Perhaps even today you believe in such things as trust and commitment. You keep all your commitments even though others don't always keep theirs. You can be trusted. If you say you will do something, you will, won't you? And basically you are fair? You wouldn't dream of meeting your own ends first. Of course not? Then why does it make you angry when someone else does not come through and fails you? Is there some hidden obligation that if you are good to others others should be good to you?

In adult years we may still expect people to meet our needs and communicate with us in just and honorable ways. Perhaps they will. Accept them if they do, but expect nothing. Deal with life, don't moralize. If others consciously or unconsciously go against your needs and values, deal with this by becoming a little wiser and more worldly in the uses of power.

For trust, substitute consciousness. A person may come through or not come through with what you consider the right behavior. Are you going to sit around lamenting your fate, or get on with the living of life?

Perhaps the greatest inhibitor to a fully vital and adult life is the betrayal that one felt in childhood and the defensive personality which was built up around this event.

Find healing in accepting that adversity is a part of being alive in this reality. We need adversity to cure us of innocence. Accept betrayal, not with unrelated forgiveness, but with an increased reality function, so that you may become truly effective in life.

There is nothing to forgive. Reality does not admit of false judgments of right and wrong. The people we at first thought good all had their shadows. You do not forgive someone or something. What happens, happens. It is done. Learn from it. That is your redemption. You learn that all people, including yourself, have shadows. You stay aware of everyone's potential for destructiveness. You accept the shadow and move on.

The Work

• What reactions are being evoked by reading the above passage? Try to get at them and express them. What attitudes have been challenged?

• What is your position on trust? How has trust actually worked in your life? How has it been effective? How has it not been effective?

• What was the great betrayal for you in childhood? Try to feel it by holding the images surrounding the betrayal in your meditative state until the feelings come out. Then process those feelings. What attitudes were being shattered at the time? What was the teaching behind the event?

• What defenses towards the possibility of new betrayal did you build up in childhood which might still be in effect today?

• There are many adults who complain that someone has betrayed them, and that it is the other person's fault that they feel badly. No one fails anyone else. We fail only ourselves. Please write about this. Perhaps there is someone still out there in your world towards whom you have anger for not being the way you wanted them to be. Try to accept them into your meditation and see-feel them both as your betrayer and your savior. Yes, savior. The goal as an adult is to take full responsibility for accepting the imperfections which come your way. If you can begin to do this you will be on your way toward accepting your own imperfections.

The only betrayal is the loss of consciousness in the face of reality.

§§§

The Anima

The image: *the bald priestess has laid her shorn hair at the foot of the altar*

"She breaks all bonds and establishes new ones."

The anima is the wild feminine energy inside every man which humbles him when he becomes too rational and too identified with his own masculine nature. She is wildly exciting, full of nuance. She is juice and mystery, acted out in fantasy, in nature, on many a couch and in many a story or poem. She breaks all bonds and establishes new ones.

The man's anima is sometimes at war with the woman's own feminine nature. For if the woman is always embodying the man's anima for him, she will be neglecting the expression of her own feminine which is sometimes different from the man's projected feminine. A man may project his feminine as a nurturing mother energy onto a woman who finds painting the most natural expression of her own feminine. If she is only concerned with embodying the man's feminine by cooking and caring for him, she will not be expressing her true feminine.

Anima projection may happen in a father-daughter relationship as well. The young woman is the young wife-woman resurrected for the father-man. Death will be approaching with the years and new young life is seen as the symbol of eternality. The father or step-father feels drawn to the young daughter. She symbolizes and acts out his feelings for him. She may manipulate him through feeling to get some of her needs met. If the projection becomes too powerful at puberty, her father, or even her brother, will turn on her. She is a woman, a sexual being they must reject for fear of incest. She who has been happy embodying the feminine then withdraws, perplexed that such beauty as she has been given has produced lust and raw anger. Anima fixation is not a happy sight.

When is the man's anima much younger than he is? If a man is attracted to younger women, if the beautiful women of his dreams are younger than he is, then his masculine conscious side is older than his feeling and feminine side. Since he has devoted so much more of his life to developing his masculine side, he has neglected his feminine, leaving it underdeveloped and immature.

For a man the way to the feminine is not by keeping the anima projected out onto certain women, but to take back the projections and develop the feeling-relational function. We integrate by turning the energy of projections into functions. This way we develop a new side of ourselves symbolized by the projection. A man who tends to project mother onto women can nurture himself, cook for himself at least once in awhile, take care of his own body instead of always needing a woman's caress to make him feel good.

On the other hand, a woman can learn not to identify totally with the anima, yet not reject evoking it. The woman who is uncomfortable with her own feminine will not be comfortable receiving the man's anima projection. She will be out of touch with this powerful aspect of relatedness between the sexes. The sexes project powerful energies onto each other, and this needs to be honored and handled with care while at the same time helping the projections be integrated.

When women feel mistreated by men they may use the power generated by the anima projection against the man to gain power over him. I will never forget seeing a beautiful friend of mine walking quickly into a coffee house with an ardent male trailing six steps behind her.

Eros is for relatedness, not power. The attractions of the sexes can be used to build beautiful and growing companionships, or they can be used in a power game of both trying to control the other. If in childhood you had to manipulate the natural projections which got evoked there, chances are you will be doing the same thing in your adult relationships. Break the chain. Integrate. Choose to be with someone who not only loves you but who integrates much of what that love can mean.

Let both sexes be guardians of the feminine.

The Work

• As a woman, what was your childhood pattern in embodying the man's anima, first with the father, or brother, and then later with boys?

• As a woman, what of your feminine have you developed for yourself that is not connected with attracting the man's anima?

• For the man, write a history of your anima. List the women you loved. Remember them all. What were the qualities which you were projecting onto these women? What realizations do you come to now?

• For the man, what of your anima projection are you now beginning to integrate and express as your own feminine side?

• For the man, did anyone in childhood accuse you of being homosexual or effeminate? What was behind it?

• For the man or woman, what were your experiences, fantasies, and attitudes about homosexuality in terms of the feminine or masculine?

• Make a plan and a commitment for dealing with the anima!

Integrating love's potential creates the ability to love.

§§§

Independence

Image: *the wolf stalks the hawk*

"I am willing to give up dependence for independence."

We may all have difficulty with this subject, even if we see ourselves as already independent.. By dealing with our compulsive dependencies, we can learn what acting with self-determining direction means.

Independence is making my own decisions about everything, not yielding to anyone else's position before first establishing consciousness of my own.

I am me. I have a separate existence from everyone else. I have a power of choice and a set of values I will not give away to someone else or to the situation itself.

We know deep in our hearts that if we do not take full responsibility for our own decisions we will regret it, we will be endangering ourselves. The truth is that if I am willing to stand up for myself, I am also giving the other person greater freedom to stand up for him or herself. If I am secure in my own position, the other person does not have to hold back on her or his position.

The birth of the ego, the choice-maker, into consciousness probably happens when the child first says No. What a moment that must be, to say No to someone else and mean it.

Too many of us have grown up saying Yes and then trying to say No later by backing out of situations or falling asleep to responsibility.

I am willing to give up dependence for independence. For I know that I can only be inter-dependent when I first come from my own sense of self. Inter-dependence means cooperation based on mutual respect for each other, balancing the power.

My affirmation is to be independent by establishing my responsibility for exercising choice and power in the world.

The Work

• If you feel you are already an independent person, check this out by evaluating your attitudes and behavior in terms of whether you let yourself be inter-dependent with others. Being independent does not mean dominating the situation, or always acting autonomously, but relating to things out of your own fullest being.

• Which are you more on the side of, saying Yes or saying No? What is behind this in terms of the dependence-independence issue?

• When do you first remember pleasing someone to get your needs met? How did this affect your later life?

Independence is functioning within the whole, rejecting nothing.

§§§

The Mother

Image: *the flowers are wilted in the vase*

"A greater parent than my personal parents wanted me to be born."

My mother seemed much a woman, although she looked like Abraham Lincoln. She had character in her beautiful face. I think of her as the one in the family who almost always came up with a perspective on life.

She considered herself a genius ever since her high school days when she passed all the exams without attending classes. She seemed an extreme introvert since she preferred to spend her time in the library reading. Having me, the unwanted child, must have been one of her greatest acts of extroversion. A more central parent than my personal parents wanted me to be born.

Memories of my mother are of a sick woman spending the time in bed drinking milk. My father would shop, go out into the world, meet people, and earn his living. My mother would stay home painting, reading, and writing poetry. Her goal was to be great, to achieve immortality through her writing. This also was my father's goal. Somehow they thought that will power plus talent would do the trick. Fame is ephemeral. It did not happen in their case. The recognition was quite minor.

I see a sickly woman afraid of life, with negative attitudes about how certain people were out to get you. Reality seemed harsh to her and she felt she had much to complain about. This has affected my own anima image in that I have been attracted to brilliant women who have problems making it in the world, creative women who are also sick with affliction.

My mother could talk for hours about the world, about literature, philosophy, art, music, politics, religion. So if my mother's focus was elsewhere, how then was my mother still a mother to me? It would be easy for me to resent her devotion to art and poetry, but my task is to look at events as they actually are so that there can be healing.

What then did my mother fulfill or not fulfill in my life at an archetypal level ?

By looking at my anima, my inner feminine, I can see what my mother constellated of the feminine archetype for me. My anima seeks the unusual and the exotic. It is concerned with spiritual things. It loves beauty. The women I have been drawn to, despite myself, have had a certain beauty, an inward look of the eyes as if dwelling much in the unconscious, and a tendency towards health problems. They have been dancers on the wheel of life, all of them. My anima also seeks women who can offer plenty of warmth and comforting. My mother didn't embody much of the nurturing side of the feminine archetype for me. She never hugged me or touched me except to shake hands when I would come home on vacation.

My mother personified the frailty of the mind when it comes to the body. I couldn't quite tell her that her theories were crazy, but they were. Just before her death she told me she was on the verge of inventing an anti-gravity machine. Myself, I am a dancer, a martial artist of sorts, vigorous and alive with good health practices. I used to become nauseous when I was too thinking. This is an obvious reaction against my mother's mental nature.

Only in Jungian analysis did I realize I hated my mother. Thank God there were other women in the world. My mother was so powerful to me, I sometimes had to hide away in myself.

My own inner feminine has developed slowly over the years. My original defensive stance against my mother created tremendous inhibition and fear of the feminine. I had no flow to me in my younger adult years. At first I could not get angry or be directly sexual with a woman. That all changed through long Jungian analysis with women analysts, inner work, conscious changes in behavior, and my relationships with women.

Our basic premise in working with childhood material is to realize that the parental archetypes within us were only partially constellated by the actual childhood parents. Our task as adults is to complete the archetype. Our compulsions, our needy child, will seek to fulfill those parts of the archetype left out in childhood. In my example I sought creative women who were also highly sexual since my mother seemed to have no sexual instincts that I could sense.

Mother, you were my inspiration and my difficulty. Now I see you with more peace in my heart because the feminine I have found is more than what you offered me. My own healing is within the archetype, not within what you gave me. You are still vivid in me but no longer the mother of my mystery.

The Work

• Everyone's mother is somewhat different, but what feelings are evoked for you from the above description? What are the problems and what are the transformations?

• Describe your experience of your own mother with particular attention to what she did and did not evoke for you. What aspects of the feminine archetype did she evoke and fulfill for you? What of the feminine was missing in your experience of her. How are you exploring new avenues of the feminine in relationships? In your inner life?

• What has been your own experience of mothering others? Are you identified with the archetype or related to it? Or both?

• Perhaps write a poem to The Mother, or paint her.

To give you must let life in.

§§§

Early Loves

Image: *in the night a flash of light seems to lose itself in the moon*

"When we're in the heat of love, we can do nothing, it seems, but go with it."

When was the last time you felt consumed by love? Early passionate love lets us know years before we can possibly integrate it that a great mystery lies behind the love experience.

Love grows and consumes us, turns us around from whatever we were doing. When we're in the heat of love, we can do nothing, it seems, but go with it. Not to have fallen deeply in love is not to have experienced the passionate longing for ultimate unity in life. Maybe it did not happen for you in the childhood years, but only came your way as a young adult? Perhaps the full passion of love has not yet occurred for you? Who can predict when our moment is to arrive. Love comes when it comes, and our choice is to say yea or nay.

Sometimes dependency and the fear of moving out into the world are so powerful it takes the overwhelming power of love to move us to a new dimension. Whenever we are stuck in our ways, watch and see if love doesn't come along to pull us up and out into the next part of our journey.

Among my first experiences there was nothing so wonderful as being in love. The women I fell in love with are powerful for me in memory to this day. I so needed what they had, the enthusiasm, the passion, the flesh and dance of life. I was falling in love with life. My ego, my conscious side, can never quite be the guide into my future, because when love flies in new doors open to what I never knew I would experience in life.

How did we handle those early loves? Did we live them out without regrets, or did we feel frustrated when they did not last?

Gradually I learned to love life itself and to love expressing my true nature. Until I have found myself, I will seek to find love in another. And while I am finding myself, I am also a lover to those whose lot it is to share with me a common destiny.

Our ability to love is our ability to live life fully. The hesitations of the young years, the sexual play, the intense talking, the songs, the dance, are all forms of self expression for feeling the vital energy of life. The more we love the freer we are to love. There are no tragedies in love if we have loved fully. The sadness of love is the unacknowledged opportunities to love we let go by without action. To love is to give soul to what life brings. When you love, love fully, conquering fear by voluntary death of the old life and by giving birth to what must be. Love knows no boundaries where the soul is at work.

The Work

• Write up your early love experiences whether they were realized or not. What feelings and dynamics were evoked for you?

• What have you learned over the years about love? Take a chance and write down a few things.

• What do you do to keep love in your life when you're not in love, or when you are not in a fulfilling love relationship? How can you feel just as creative about your life?

• Describe someone you have been in love with. Then translate their qualities into dynamics within yourself which you can live more fully in your life.

• Watch out for neurosis! It is the death of love. Find your early love trauma and transform it, or your ability to love will weaken. Neurosis makes us love those who are not right for us but who evoke our love wounds and the need for healing. How then do you use love for personal healing?

Love lives where the heart is made free.

§§§

Sex

Image: *bells in the night ringing*

". . . the yoni and lingam are one."

In certain cultures children are allowed an almost uninhibited expression of sexuality. But for most of us our sexual feelings and expression have been colored with moral, ethical and collective considerations. Our parents and our society may have visited upon us all sorts of dire forebodings about sex. We are not only left to carry the sexual energy given to each one of us in life, but we also have to drag around extra fears, traumas and attitudes around the sexuality.

If extra burdens have been added to our sexual lives then let us use sex to free us of those burdens. Fear of the negative hardly leads to being positive. Transforming the negative gives us hope. Note the following attitudes. These are hardly absolutes, but to the young person's mind what are merely attitudes seem like the last word of God visited on them by the parents.

> • It is wrong for a child to masturbate • It is wrong to masturbate • It is wrong to masturbate in front of one's lover • It is wrong to go naked in public • It is wrong to have sex in public • It is wrong to have group sex • It is wrong to have sex when you should be working •

For contrast, note these "adult" attitudes which are commonly accepted as positive. They show that while they attack healthy sexuality, the serious issues of life go mostly unchallenged.

> • It is all right to drink and get drunk in public • It is all right to make money off of another person • It is right to kill men, women and children who belong to the enemy • It is all right to lie to one's associates • It is right to sometimes lie to one's spouse • It is right to hate others on this earth •

These are all attitudes, not absolutes, but they show vividly the contrast between the forces for life and the forces for death at work in the psychic of every person on this earth.

Back in childhood the sexual force began to grow in power while the adults sought to repress it in us, unless they were enlightened themselves about the act of love. Instead of letting sexual love remain pure in itself, the adults heaped excess baggage onto it. We return to childhood to see what that baggage was. We return to childhood to throw the baggage over the nearest cliff. The worst you can do in life is pass on your baggage to the next generation. Let us find renewal and fulfillment in our sexuality, and not trauma. Most adults have trauma and life-defeating attitudes around their sexuality which no amount of sexual exercises, sex manuals, or porno flicks will overcome.

The healing way is not simply to get uninhibited by expressing sex, but to free oneself of the legacy of the past. What was it that your parents did to you that still hurts you today in regard to your sexuality? What sexual attitudes were you taught at any early age which act like knives against the fiber of your soul?

Sex is not only sex, it is mystery, the life force, renewal, and the source of our creativity and affection. Use it well in and out of relationship. Find wealth in the possibility for new unity daily. Do not die before the grave gets you. You are your own best lover. Be good to yourself and throw off the past. Yes, there is risk, but not disaster. Even the worst, if truly lived, is life.

The Work

• Describe your earliest experience of sexuality. What negative attitudes may have been formulated in your experience and how might you transform them?

• What attitudes did you pick up in childhood about your own sexuality? What have been their effects on your life?

• Describe the beauty and grace in a childhood sex experience. How might you draw upon it today? What is sexuality for you now?

• For your sacred area you can make clay representations of the female and male genitalia, as was the ancient practice in most religions. In India they called the female opening the yoni and the male thruster the lingam. In divine ecstasy the yoni and lingam are one.

Sex is God-play in the flesh.

§§§

Relatedness-Intimacy

Image: *a new configuration of stars in the sky*

". . . to be related I must yield my necessity to prevail."

Relatedness is going towards others and opening to them as much of oneself as they can handle. Relatedness is also accepting and allowing others to approach and share with you some of their real selves. In relatedness we form bonds which enhance new life.

Non-relatedness is preserving my space against all challenges. Non-relatedness is my viewpoint prevailing in all situations, being right no matter what. Non-relatedness is not honoring the other person's perspective, is seeing the world through one's eyes alone. Even if I feel right in the situation, to be related I must yield my necessity to prevail.

Relationship is often not easy to achieve. From childhood onward we have defended ourselves against the universe and everyone around us. If I have a defensive personality, I am not capable of relatedness, and therefore relationship. If most of the time I feel more related to my objects than to those who would be close to me, I have little skill for relatedness.

Fear of intimacy also limits relationship. When we are about to become close to each other, one of us will throw in a conflict to split us apart. We want intimacy, yet we fear it. The way out? To come out of the protective castle into the real world where things hurt and things are wonderful.

Why do we hold onto our positions for so long? What a burden we give ourselves in having to defend our views about everything. If someone else has the better viewpoint in the situation, why not feel relieved? It takes so much energy always having to be right. All I want to do is live life richly, and the more you can contribute to our mutual journey, the better. Not having to be right also frees me to make a stronger contribution to our relationship.

In childhood most people have experienced parents who had to be right. By always being the ultimate authority parents neglect their job to be a supportive resource for their children. So as parents tried to control them the children tried to defend themselves. In adult life people relate to others the way they were related to as children. Controlled children make controlling lovers. Controlling lovers create defensive and attacking lovers.

Greater suffering resides in having to defend oneself than in opening oneself to intimacy and life. Opening to life and intimacy will cause the weak and egocentric to leave, but in their place will come others of stronger fiber. Remember, not others with your point of view necessarily. There may be fewer potential friendships the more deeply the journey goes. But what is lost in number will increase in communion with yourself and with those who count. When you open doors to the heart, many will want to enter, but few still will pay the price for such intimacy. We pay for intimacy by our willingness to change within the communion created by honesty and love.

The Work

• List the ways you became defensive in childhood rather than relational. What were you defending yourself against? Now list the ways you may still be defensive in adult life. What new ways of dealing with relatedness are there that you will commit yourself to trying out?

• List ways you have changed over the years to allow more and more intimacy. What were the causes of those changes?

• How might you have given up on relationship, not the need for relationship, but on your commitment to learning how to have fulfilling relationships? Search deeply within for those patterns and attitudes which may be defeating your willingness to be relational at a deep level. Challenge your intimates in terms of intimacy and relatedness.

Intimacy creates relationship and relationship creates life.

§§§

Power

Image: *the child sits surrounded by peers*

"The baby directs energy to get its needs met."

Power. What is power to a little child? Do the parents have all the power? What are the first uses of power by the child?

Power is energy. Or better yet, power is directed energy. The small child knows how helpless he or she is and must test the limits of reality to see where the power lies. Few parents can stand to have their children screaming and crying for long periods. Thus power comes into play. The baby directs energy to get its needs met.

What happens when the child begins growing up? Perhaps there is a constant struggle over power. It is not important nutritionally whether the child eats everything on the plate, but in many families it is important who wins the contest. Whose value is to be followed? Whose value wins out? The one with the greatest power to enforce it?

Certainly the most healthy family situation is one in which a balance of power is maintained most of the time. Did you grow up in a family in which your parents willingly allowed you to have some power? Did they yield their values, needs and wishes sometimes in order to go along with you? Of course they did, if you had loving, secure and conscious parents.

Or was it an ongoing struggle in the family to win power away from the parents? Or was the situation the other extreme in which your parents would yield to you on almost anything? If the parents are too yielding, then the child cannot find boundaries, the containers of power which we call reality.

There are those who would rather look out on the world and criticize its wrongs without ever creating power to correct them. And there are those who consider values to be ephemeral and arbitrary, and therefore focus mainly on increasing their power without much thought for how it is used.

Thus we have the power-seekers versus the idealists. Which side are you habitually on? Did you retreat as a child and remain critical of those around you? Was the world beneath you? Or did you think that in order not to get squashed you had to go for whatever power was available to you?

These questions are important because in order for us to be effective as adults in this life we must have power. The more power we have the more we will be able to change reality. But power also needs context in order to be fully effective. Power which focuses on itself will defeat itself. Yet power expressed within the natural principles of the universe can be extremely effective.

As adults, are we willing to go for power and use it to manifest true values in this reality? That is the real question. If we are not, we have probably been maimed in childhood in some great power struggle with the parents or family. Transformation is needed for the adult to use power, energy, money, influence, love, to create a renewed and revitalized life for oneself and others.

The Work

• Pick two or three questions from the above text and work with them. Which questions would you like to avoid?

• Describe the power dynamics in your living situation when you were growing up. If there were stages, describe them.

• How, specifically, did you seize and withdraw from power?

• As an adult, what is your stance on power? How can you be more comfortable and effective with it?

Power without consciousness destroys itself.
Consciousness without power lacks effectiveness.

§§§

The Family Neurosis

Image: *the wagon wheel lies broken*

"I could redeem my life. I could feel again."

In the family closet a neurosis lies hidden. Every family has a skeleton in the closet, the gaping wound closed over and hidden from public view, the family embarrassment.

Each generation passes on some form of the family neurosis to the next until someone chooses to make the anomaly conscious and transform it. Who wants children if we are going to plaster them with what our parents put over on us? Do we want to allow the maiming of our own child by our own hand?

My family on my father's side went through the pogroms of Russia at the turn of the century. The Cossacks ransacked, raped and killed the Jews. The terror created and intensified neurosis among the people. My father's generation of five children migrated to America with my grandparents. They never sought therapy. It was too new for them. They sought, instead, power, money, wealth, effectiveness and freedom. But what did they know about bringing up children to be healthy? Each of my own generation went into therapy. I myself have had fifteen years of it. I worked hard. I learned that I could redeem my life. I could feel again.

It must be strange for a small child to be born into someone's living myth, the adversaries, the coldness, the strange behavior and wild views about reality.

This generation seeks therapy, understanding, and change so that their children are not burdened by problems other than their own. If not for oneself, we can change at least for our child's sake. We do not perceive yet what the new children will be like who have had a more conscious generation of parents. The weight of the generations is immense. Yet the greatest force on earth may be the healing power of consciousness, a power which can break decisively the chain of the family neurosis which has taken generations of denial to build and years of personal therapy to destroy and redeem.

The Work

• What were some of the things in your family which people tried to keep hidden from you? What was your reaction to this? What sort of pattern is behind what was kept secret?

• How does the family neurosis show up in you? How are you a bit extreme in the same way? Or how are you an opposite to the family?

• How did your parents deal with the family neurosis? Did they reinforce it or fight it? What effect has this had on you?

• How would you say your wound or neurosis affects your children, or need to have or not to have children?

• What are you doing to stop the family neurosis in your generation?

We can defeat ourselves with our own blood.

§§§

The Friends We Had

Image: *the tree has lost its branches*

". . . seeing ever anew the rainbow in relationship and the broken bridges needing repair."

When I was around ten I had a friend named Ron. I think he was taller than I and red headed like myself. Once a year we would have a great big fight, crying, screaming, and wrestling each other to the ground, trying to make the other give up. That was true friendship! He was my closest friend for many years. We would go off into the woods every afternoon after school, build forts, and dam up small streams. In the Fall, we would steal corn from the field and roast it on our outdoor, hidden fire.

When I went to military school at age thirteen that part of childhood ended. Somewhere in those early teen years I met a friend at a summer camp whose name was Israel. We climbed the mountain together and sat on the moss overlooking the valley of farmland, the neat fields of different colors, the future laid out before us. Yes, the future. Israel and I talked long about the future. We were close. We thought big thoughts. A sensitivity developed between us, an imperceptible aura of destiny. We had great ideas. We were nubile, not quite ready, but not yet encumbered by life. I saw Israel years later. He called me out of the blue. He had been to medical school and was professionally established. The glow was still there between us but we didn't quite hit it off. There is no recapturing childhood in an outer sense. My thoughts, my feelings, are of a different world long since gone down the path of long ago.

I shared the first mysteries of sex with Denise, Ron's sister. I was twelve and she eleven and we both found ourselves locked up in an isolation ward at the school infirmary with chicken pox. We made a house under the bed. I took off my pajamas. She lifted up her shift. We were scared of the nurses and thrilled by our secret activity. My mother visited me and I felt so guilty about my friend. One day before I left that school, I was running through the fields in summertime and suddenly there was Denise with flowers in her hand. We looked at each other long and hard and then one of us ran away.

> A friend is someone I can be real with • A friend is someone I have shared the deepest moments of life with • A friend is the witness in some essential part of my life • Come forward, my friend, and we will create the meaning of our lives • To be a friend is as much to be needed as to need • To be a friend is to practice love, compassion and anger, to delight where there is play, and to pound on the door when things have gone astray • A friend is laughter, love and pain, is the sudden recognition, seeing ever anew the rainbow in relationship and the broken bridges needing repair • I have chosen you, my friend. Is it your choice as well?

We let go of the past by taking the essence with us. My boyhood friends seemed vital to me. With them I glimpsed my own future and thought I was seeing theirs. Ah, the intense moments! It would take the years and steady work to even come that close again to the raw germ of life again!

The Work

• Please write feelingly about your early childhood friendships or lack of them. What kind of person were you as based on your friendships? What kind of person were you attracted to in your friendships?

• Do you tend to have friends of the same sex or of the opposite sex? How do you explain your propensity? What might you do to balance things out?

• Review your present friendships using the following criteria. Is the friendship two-way and balanced? Do you get as much as you give? Do you give as much as you get? Is what you have in common central to the relationship? If not why are you relating? Are you being more and more open with your feelings, and is your friend opening up likewise? Are you keeping the friendship continuing past its dying point? Are you afraid if you let the friendship go there will not be another to take its place?

We relate to others to relate to ourselves.

§§§

Abuse

Image: *lightning strikes in the cave*

"Every healing needs a wound."

We were called into the main room of the cottage where thirty of us boys lived, ages ten to twelve and told to remain silent by the older boys who supervised us. I looked over at my friend Ron. Our eyes met, but neither of us said a word. We both knew better than to make ourselves conspicuous at this time. An older, stronger boy looked us over and said one of the boys had had some money stolen and they wanted to find out who did it. Stealing was not uncommon in the charity school to which I had been confined since age six. I myself never stole. I played the good boy, and would play the good boy again this day. But I had at times tried to find the thief myself by hiding and observing suspicious children, forgetting for the moment that I was also a child. We knew of one boy who was a habitual stealer, but he was not taking the blame for this one, too bad for all of us.

The older boys had us lie on our backs and raise our legs off the floor and keep them there. With threats and insults they terrorized us until the pain seemed unbearable. Nobody confessed, so that we all had to endure the torture and the fear. Then they took us one by one into a room and confronted us individually with shouts and pushes.

"Did you do it! Did you do it!" they shouted to each of us alone in that room with the upperclassmen. I played my most innocent self and so only got shouts and shoves. Another boy who had stolen in the past we found out later had been picked up and thrown against the radiator. The terror was extreme and this and many other incidents like this made me so repressed that finally I showed no feelings and kept and extremely even and subdued voice in everything, a voice which never changed until after many years of therapy. My insecurities burned me. My defense was to hide in invisibility. My rages were secret, even to myself.

Another time when I was older and now residing at a military school, the upperclassmen called certain of us out in the night to punish us for a wrong we had not done. I was made to pull down my undershorts and received many hard and stinging blows with a large wooden paddle. I wanted to throw the table over on the boy in charge, but my fear was greater than my anger. I was too inhibited to fight back, to take anger and run with it. I felt the situation as totally unfair. I felt impotent, insecure, lonely, helpless. I wanted revenge.

Abuse is the norm, is the great Adversary Archetype entering the child's life. Abuse comes by violence and by sexual misdeeds. We as children are victimized by those stronger than ourselves, it is our lot to be a victim to these great misuses of power. Better to learn in childhood that you are not all-powerful and that sometimes no one is there to help you in your time of need. As adults we cry out and hurt over the abuses we have suffered, but do we also accept them as natural? Am I to say that I should not have been severely terrorized as a boy? No, I cannot say that, I cannot go against reality. Beware the attitude which says that things should have been different than they were. For fundamental to receiving the blows of adversity is also the recognition that no matter how difficult the circumstance we are also given the resources for self-healing and transformation.

The unrealistic attitude is to say that such-and-such should never happen to a child. It did happen and that is reality. To expect the good to triumph over evil, the hero to always win out over the adversary, is to cling to unrealistic attitudes and expectations. To accept adversity as natural is to become real to this life as it is.

Yes, of course I was beaten as a child. That is what certain people with power do to their victims. Yes, I was also sexually molested, but so what? Yes, I was forced to build an enormous defense system against the terror, but so what? What is crucial is that I also found the resources to transform the wounds done to me, to collapse the defense system and begin to live a healed and renewed life. Every healing needs a wound. Each of us will need to feel the Great Wound in childhood and try to defend against it. Then in adult life we can work it through and live differently. We can heal the wound of childhood by dissolving the defense system and living a transforming life in tune with the healing center of the Self.

The Work

• What was the form of abuse you went through in childhood? It may have been overt, either sexual or violent, or more hidden, even the wound of missing love and a fundamental understanding of who you were.

• Having described your childhood abuse experience, then describe the defense system you built to defend yourself against further abuse. Is this defense system still in operation today? How?

• Choose to let go of your defense system and move into a stance of dealing with anything which comes your way. If you are still a complainer or a rager, then you have not left your defensive personality yet. If you think there should not be evil in the world, then you still need work on your attitudes to make them realistic. Reality is healing. Idealism causes defeat and despair.

• Rewrite your early abuse trauma with a more healing outcome. This changes patterns deep inside. Let the full force of adversity rain down upon your childhood head, but this time deal with it more resiliently instead of repressing hurt or turning invisible.

• You have described what the trauma and defense pattern was in childhood. Now see how this pattern operates in your adult life. Then create alternate and healing ways for dealing with adversity today.

What we flee from we become .

§§§

Egocentricity

Image: *a cracked egg lying at the edge of a table*

"The way to get what you want is to not want it."

Not one of us is always fun to be with. We each have our little foibles, our egocentricities which drive others up the wall.

We are egocentric when we act in ways to build up our own egos at the expense of others or of life. We are egocentric when we do not trust a larger process than ourselves, when we try to control, to get our own way in everything. We are egocentric when we act defensively and withdraw, or make ourselves unnecessarily unavailable to others. We are ego-centric when we try to put everyone else's house in order but our own.

Fritz Kunkle, an American psychologist writing in the 1950's, describes four types of egocentricity. Two are developed by growing up in a harsh environment, and the other two result from growing up in a soft environment.

> The Star grows up in a soft environment and shows a marked extroversion. A Star wants the center of the stage • The Clinging Vine grows up in a soft environment and shows a marked introversion. This type depends on others • The Bully grows up extroverted in a harsh environment. The Bully's response to difficulty is to try to dominate, no matter what the consequences • A Turtle grows up introverted in a harsh environment, with the tendency to withdraw in the face of adversity.

As described, these are essentially negative and defensive reactions to reality. The Star feels insecure if not the center of stage and so tries to dominate with talent and energy, creating love. The Bully tries to dominate with power and aggression, creating fear. The Clinging Vine tries to dominate by neediness, creating concern. The Turtle tries to dominate by withdrawal, creating compulsion in others to break through.

The positive aspects of the above dispositions lie in their transformations. Behind each is a natural personality quality useful in life. There is a time to be creatively alone like a turtle, a time to be vulnerable like a clinging vine, a time to be expressive and "out there" like a star, and a time to be assertive like a bully or strong person. The transformation is in letting go of the defense system and living each of the dynamics appropriately as part of our own wholeness.

We look at our egocentricities to further study the nature of our defense systems produced in childhood, and to see their effects in adult life. How do each of us as adults tend to react to situations? If we do not know, ask our friends to type us. They know! To act defensively in adult life is usually not appropriate and prevents relationship.

In terms of early childhood dynamics the child develops ego by focusing on its own needs and wants. It gathers possessions. It chooses for itself more than for others. This is a necessary stage towards self-autonomy. Once a child has established his autonomy he will outgrow the need to focus so much energy on himself. If, however, this need for self-affirmation has been thwarted the egocentric child will become an egocentric adult.

In the adult years to always choose first for oneself means that we will be offensive and even hurtful towards others. We will remain subjective and not objectively choose what is best for all in a given situation. We will antagonize others needlessly and have little in the way of fulfilling relationships. As adults we learn that we do not exist alone and are inter-dependent with others. We learn to choose for others as well as for ourselves. The cure of egocentricity is to put oneself in alignment with source energies greater than oneself, and in so doing we are being fed the vital stuff of life.

The Work

• Make a list of your egocentricities and how you will transform them. Make also a list of a friend's egocentricities as you see them and share.

• Type yourself! Star? Clinging Vine? Bully? Turtle? What was your dominant in childhood? Has it changed with the life transitions? What are its positive aspects?

• What would be the positive aspects of transforming your egocentricity?

   If we were not accepted as children we will not as adults accept others.

§§§

The Defense System

Image: *the castle walls are cracking*

"I was far from the good person I hoped to be in order to get along in the world."

My defense system developed in a harsh boarding school environment where I received little warmth, understanding, or love. At times I played the bully. At times I withdrew. I repressed my feelings so much that my voice became even in tone to not betray emotion. If I showed anger or fear in childhood, there was a good possibility I would be beaten by one of the older boys. Being in a prison is how I think of my childhood schools. I became a warden to my own feelings. I would hurt inside but never show it. I would hide within my own secret thoughts.

Later in adult intimate relationships with women, my feelings and my anger would poke out. I had great fear of being rejected. And I played the bully. I thought that now at last in the warmth of adult sexuality I could get what I wanted. But in fear of not getting what I wanted, I would be demanding and try to make things happen. I was so defensive that even the smallest things would upset me. And since I was getting upset, others were upset with me as well. I was a difficult person to handle.

I was most defensive at a time when I thought most highly of myself. God knows I could not be wrong in any situation. I was not angry. I was not being unkind. The trouble existed in the other person. In therapy I chose to own my own shadow and not defend myself against it, but to accept and take it in, however embarrassed I felt. I was learning to recognize that being upset with someone means not that they are wrong, but that I have feelings and needs which are making an attempt to reveal themselves. Embarrassment is due to the ego-identification with the persona being suddenly shattered, throwing the person into their shadow.

My transformation came in letting my feelings out and becoming more direct in expressing myself and my needs. I realized I did not have to get what I wanted if I could express what I wanted. Not expressing my needs led to agony because I defeated myself in not asserting my wants and desires.

It is freeing to go from a defensive to an accepting personality. It took years of confrontation and soul-searching, both in therapy and in relationships, to accept my egocentricity and my shadow. I was far from the good person I hoped to be to get along in the world. I found that the more vulnerable I became in a human way, the closer I got to people and the closer they got to me. My defensiveness had created distances which almost nobody could bridge. Now there was hope. I was willing to lie awash in a sea of blood and see if anyone would respond, even take care of me.

Although nobody came forward to care for me, my close associates and friends joined me with their own vulnerability. We became companions in the end. We worked side by side, each tending our own wounded, inner child. And that makes me laugh, and cry.

The defense system is a set of attitudes and behavior we built up to repress feelings evokes by other people's aggression and even love. Instead of expressing our feelings and needs directly, we learn to manipulate situations and people in order to get some of our needs met. We act defensively. We live in anxiety and hide our vulnerability from ourselves and the world. We lose our energy and became rigidly locked into our defenses, thus stifling the spontaneity of life and feeling. We rule our castle through our own worst egocentricities. We feel alienated and in danger of losing our humanity until at last we choose to leave the defensive personality, suffer the transformation, and live at last joyously open in grounded and exciting ways. We commit ourselves to consciously processing whatever comes up in life.

The Work

• How would you describe, free flow, your own defense system?

• How might you begin to transform your defense system? What role does commitment play here? What would be some creative alternatives to having a defense system? Do we also accept our own defensiveness?

• What is the alternative to living defensively? Are you willing to let go, to risk, to live fully, dealing with everything as it comes along? If not, what is stopping you? Most likely it is your defense system which imprisons you as you attempt to shut out part of your world.

We defend against that which we are unwilling or unable to process.

§§§

Ego

Image: *the ball is thrown through the center of the circle*

"No one can make our choices for us. The consequences we suffer alone."

The birth from childhood into adulthood is the birth of the creative ego. To leave home is to leave behind letting others make decisions for you. You do want to go out in the world, don't you? You do want to make decisions for yourself, to sink or swim based on the actions you take? You are not afraid, are you, that you will make the wrong choice in something and have to pay for it yourself? Where are the parents in adult life to bail us out? If we screw up in a major relationship, or are out of work, we can always come home, can't we? If we run out of money the parents will offer a loan or a gift, won't they?

Symptoms of a weak ego? Yes. We have spent all of childhood, unless we were wonderfully trained, relying on our parents and others in authority to suggest the right choices for us. Sometimes the only areas where we as young people could assert our own authority and choice-making power was in our hidden sex life or in the taking of drugs. Otherwise, the parents tried to control us, tried to tell us what to do, where to go to college, what to work at, what kind of friends we should have. This is of course terrible training in making choices. It is not the content of the decision making which is crucial but the process itself of choices and their consequences.

• To build a strong ego is to take responsibility for one's own choices and their consequences. • The true adult chooses her or his own lovers • Pays her way in life • Does not follow a guru or any teacher who requires the giving up of choice-making power • Does not allow one's relational partner to veto power over one's own choice-making • Does not rely on friends for advice in how to act in life • Does not remain ambivalent in the face of life choices needing to be made • Does not follow psychics, astrologers, therapists, and so forth, who tell one who to be with and what to choose in life •

• The strong adult relishes the tension between opposites as opportunities for conscious choice-making • Is decisive when necessary, or flowing when openness is required • Chooses as quickly as the occasion demands • Actualizes the potentials of life when ripe through choice and action rather than waiting in fear and therefore missing the moments of greatest opportunity • Puts the ego in the service of deeper sources than ego so that choices may be well made and lead to fulfillment for those involved whenever possible •

Use the above characteristics for your own perspective on how you are doing. Prepare to graduate from childhood by more and more making your own choices in everything that you do.

The great break-through in choice-making seems to occur in the late teenage years. It is then that most children realize that their parents no longer have superior wisdom and cannot make the right choices others. Until this transition point, say age seventeen, the young adult sees problems as coming from "out there." The parents or the school, or whatever, want certain things. One is rewarded or blamed by others according to what one does.

The perspective changes as the young person realizes that success will depend, not on others, but on what he or she chooses and does in life. "Making the grade" becomes a choice, not luck or pressure from outside. The pressures are still there but the approach is now more through choice. I choose to learn, to study, to seek work, to have my own kind of friends, and so it goes.

The birth of the ego, of the independent choice-making function combined with a self-image of making it on one's own in the world, sets in. Some enter adulthood living in a self-determining, choicefull way. Others, who were never trained to choose, enter a sexual or a religious relationship to maintain dependency, allowing others to take authority and make their choices for them. This hardly works in the long run. No one can make our choices for us. The consequences we suffer alone.

The Work

• Write a short history of your own growth in choice-making and ego self-determination starting in childhood. What is the pattern there? What issues have you solved so far? What issues are left to work on?

• Describe yourself in terms of the chief creative ego characteristics of choice-making, self-determination, inner authority, independence, realistic image of oneself, ability to be effective and self-sustaining in life, and conscious awareness of yourself and others on a daily basis. Which of these characteristics did you achieve in childhood, and which are you achieving now in your adult life?

The ego works on ego to become ego.

§§§

Healing

Image: *the serpent swallows its own tail*

"We are sick in adult life because the wounds of childhood are crying out in us."

When I was at my first boarding school from age six to age twelve I would get sick every year or so with vomiting and dizziness so that they would have to send me to the infirmary for a couple of days. This was a small hospital of twelve beds where you got to stay overnight to be watched over by the young nurses. They would always make a fuss over me and give me ginger ale to cure my vomiting. I had to be sick to get some healing. The cold environment of boarding school was killing off any human warmth in me and I needed at long intervals to know that personal caring and love did exist in the world. My stay at the infirmary would then balance out my psyche and I could go back to the dorms to endure further suffering until I could finally escape from childhood into adult life.

We all have a need for healing, so this becomes one of our primary issues in life. Not only do we have minor illnesses throughout our lives but many of us achieve a major illness or two, some of which even kill us. It is quite possible that what motivates all illness, physical and mental, is that original wound from childhood which was not healed and transformed. We are sick in adult life because the wounds of childhood are crying out in us.

To heal is to bring resolution to a split, a malfunctioning in the psyche and in the body. When we are sick certain organs are not working in their characteristic way. They are blocked, they are resisting the natural energy flow of life. Sometimes the old tissue or mental patterning must be cut out of the surround so that other functioning can continue. This is the radical step of eliminating the old and the useless. Healing is a protective act of eliminating the destructive.

The other face of healing is that which transforms. Again the pattern or organ is blocking energy, is refusing to be a part of the whole. We attempt to evoke healing or resolution here by accepting the wounded part instead of resisting it. Healing brings the part back within the whole. A change in how energy is moved through the part occurs and the whole is itself transformed by including the part.

All trauma is originally a blow to the natural functioning of the organism. In reaction, the organism seeks to protect itself by building a defense system around the wound. We act defensively to prevent further blows from hurting us. In order to heal we must allow the defense system to be breached, the wound must be cut open and suctioned of its poisoning effect. as trauma is again exposed. The wounded one goes through the trauma again, but without defending against it this time. The full experience of being wounded is accepted as an energy to be dealt with rather than resisted. Resolution is evoked instead of defensiveness. The wound heals because it is brought within the whole. The whole functions again at full capacity because all of its parts are working together, none resisting or blocking the other.

This model applied to severe cases of trauma, such as child abuse, rape, accident, and war atrocity, means that the sufferer would be guided through the experience emotionally with enactments, visualization, dreamwork, and a feeling process. Energy is released from the repression and new life is possible. Being abused in childhood is not a life-long tragedy if worked with in depth. Everyone has adversity to deal with in some form. Staying angry, hurt, and ineffective over one's wounds becomes indulgence at a certain point if transition is not made. We choose to experience the wound fully, then we choose to get out of the wound and live non-defensively but openly with a fresh creativity about life. I have seen this process work many times for myself and those I have done therapy with. When healing occurs we feel it as one of the great events of life.

The Work

• Using the above description, take yourself through a healing process around some trauma of childhood still affecting you today.

• Describe how to deal with hurts in a non-defensive yet protective and integrative and whole way.

Healing the wound wounds the healer.

§§§

First Sexual Experience–

Traumatic

Image: *the rose has fallen, the petals scattered*

"We do not redeem the dark side by avoiding it, but by encountering it fully."

Our first sexual experiences color the rest of our lives.

The following true to life stories may be upsetting to you. Certain specifics can clash with your attitudes or evoke your shadow. Please deal with it. These cases are described exactly how they happened, and in each there followed healing and redemption.

She was seventeen, attractive, but did not think well of herself. She considered herself ugly and definitely not popular, and so when the boy she knew asked her out and insisted on having his way with her she finally gave in. It was love of some sort, she reasoned, but it was also rape, and this cut through her heart. Now at age thirty she is dealing with tremendous insecurities based on fear of being invaded.

He was around eight years old when an uncle sodomized his mouth. The man was ugly in action and in appearance. In spite of this, the boy grew up to be a man sensitive to love. He adopted a gay life-style, and was attracted to young men. They had beautiful bodies, but though the sex was good the humiliation he secretly felt made him uneasy. In dream therapy he found how the original childhood trauma had colored his adult years. He liked women but was drawn to men. He realized with a shock that he was trying to redeem the original ugly experience of violation by giving fellatio to beautiful young men. He found that he no longer had to do this because in therapy he went through the trauma of the rape, expressed his rage and hurt, and then on his own made the choice to include women in his intimate life.

Can you as reader take one more severe example of what happens to children when sexuality is off?

> She was seventeen and a virgin. She went out on a date with a boy from another town. He took her to his apartment to change his clothes and there forced himself sexually upon her. She submitted reluctantly, hardly knowing what to do. She was afraid of his violence. She was not in touch with her own anger and felt helpless. Years later after she sought help in therapy she came to dream therapy because she was dreaming of dark males who would cause extreme fear in her without doing anything overt. She related to men but was afraid of them. Her dream therapy involved going through the trauma of the rape again in a two-hour guided reentry. I played the male, playing all males in interacting with her. The rage, the anger, the sensitivity, the hurt came out. She said what she needed to say to her adversary this time around. She acknowledged how she had been robbed of a positive first sexual experience. She let it go, and I let go to the healing energy. Soon after this she met the right man for her, allowed herself to be open and vulnerable, they married, and she had her children and family at last.

We do not redeem the dark side by avoiding it, but by encountering it fully. The only redemption is in what can be different now. We cannot change the past but we can live differently in the future. Even a bad first sexual experience and its effects can be transformed. Some will be born to sex through adversity, and some through love. One is more painful. The other more joyful, if more innocent. The good as well as the bad can become an addiction, so ultimately it is what you do with sex that counts. Make your sexual life conscious, however it develops, and you will be more likely to integrate it into the rest of your life.

The Work

• Write up or describe your first traumatic sexual experience with yourself or with another. What is the pattern emerging from this, and how has it affected the rest of your life, sexually and otherwise?

• Certain attitudes must have been generated by your early sexual experiences. What are these attitudes, and what are their effects on you? Which need changing? What can be more whole attitudes to replace the old ones?

• What are some ways you can work on releasing the trauma you may have around sex? To become sexual is to let go to and create with the life force. It's just that all sorts of other stuff gets in the way. What is in the way of your own sexuality?

• For redemption, in a meditative state create for yourself a healing first sexual experience. Try to get into it at a feeling and image level. Perhaps masturbate with it also, or play-act it with a good lover.

• Find the child in you who has never grown up sexually and welcome him or her into the fold.

The blade of reality cuts as deep as love.

§§§

First Sexual Experience–

Positive

Image: *a ring lies out on a velvet cushion*

"There are many ways to live but only one way to die."

The first sexual experience is for some a fulfilling one, one in which the two people genuinely love each other to the extent they can. They learn together. One is not raped and the other is not the aggressor. Their opening to each other is gradual and mutual. They share in other ways besides sexually. And when they finally are without clothes together and freely expressing the caring, wild energy of mating, they are safe, they are in love, they are joyful in what life can be.

Such an experience will not last forever, of course. Kisses are sweeter than wine, as the song goes, but wine, the heaviness of life, may come in and end that which seemed so close to paradise.

The following is a positive example of the choice to love.

> She was all of eighteen, a warm and passionate young woman who nevertheless had not had sexual intercourse. She had dated several boys. Some had pushed for more. They were the wrong ones. They lacked subtlety, finesse. Then she met him. He was older than she by a few years. He was experienced, and yet not that experienced. He had not known a full relationship until he met her. She had deep feelings for him. They went through ups and downs, the splits due to parental pressure, the getting back together again in secret. They kissed passionately, talked all the time, went to the beach a lot, and to other places in nature, danced at the folk dances.

One day they were finally naked together. She almost felt herself ready to have him, her first man. He hesitated. They did other loving things. He wasn't sure why, but he was scared. Perhaps he didn't want her to open up to other men after him? He knew he did not want to lose her.

Then in early spring she came over in the afternoon to his house when his roommates were away at work and school. The rain fell gently with a moist fragrance. The morning glories outside his windows looked lush in their purples and pinks. He had resolved in his own mind what he would do. He was making a commitment. She had her own key to the house and let herself in. He was under the covers in bed in his back room. She knelt by his side and kissed him, and he invited her to take off her clothes and climb in bed with him. They felt warm and cozy together, warm with caring, joy, the quiet spring afternoon, warm with love passion as they kissed and rubbed together. She thought that he was stimulating her like so many times before, arousing her to the warm releases that made them both sing inside. His mind was resolved as he slowly with each stroke penetrated her. To be fully inside for the first time seemed so special as he felt himself deep within the depths of her lovely being.

He told her he was in all the way and she woke from her passion in surprise and realized that yes, they were completely connected, yes, they were as one, they were intimate and excited with each other. The fires of their mutual life which had so long been smoldering now took off lifting them both beyond themselves into the realms of ecstatic being, the great passion whose fruit is love.

It was her first time. Now the evening was arriving and the natural light took on a softer glow. He saw her there all naked in the mirror looking at herself, tears rolling down her cheeks. He held her as she let go, an infinite sadness, a new opening to life. For by this birth their death would also come. He had been offered one of the great gifts of his life-time, and he had given her with caring her first full experience of love, a safe experience, a feeling experience, a letting go to life. She looked so dusky there in the mirror against his lighter skin. Their bodies and their being revealed in the mirror on the wall of time.

He made up a poem for her and for their love there in front of the mirror before they dressed, before they moved on to eat, to talk, to live. She looked to see how she was now different after the full love-making. She would later walk around on campus with a new secret. She had a lover, a man in her, a new step in life as a full woman. The love they kindled finally led to marriage, to more love, to divorce, to new love, to children, to divorce, to new life. The wheel of death and birth moves always forward. Adversity follows fortune, as misfortune is the prelude to new life.

This life episode is used to show what a major transition can be like if it is freely chosen at the right time in the right place. But simply having a positive experience of transition did not make life any easier. In some ways the positive experience is less a preparation for life than the negative one.

We who journey with wholeness as a commitment learn to take both the positive and the negative in equal stride. The good things need as much healing as the bad. But who would dare take the beautiful experiences away from us? To experience beauty is to experience wholeness. We know how far we have fallen if, once having found life, we cannot choose it passionately over and over again, even in the midst of severe adversity.

Return to childhood then, to those beginnings and transitions wherein we first learned to drink of life, and find there what it is to live out the pattern, to desire fullness instead of decrease, to desire wholeness instead of dwelling in splits and one-sidedness, to choose life in the fullness with which it comes to us.

The Work

• Write up your own experience of sexual transition. It can be with another or alone, late or early. It was a significant moment of your life. Relate to it now for its essence.

• To heal a negative first sexual experience, face the trauma and the defense system it produced in you. Then go on to recreate in your own sacred imagination what would be the most healing first sexual experience you could have had. This resets the archetypes within you, freeing you to express more fully the life force in sex and other activities.

• How have you lived up to the potential of your first positive sexual experience? What kind of person are you as seen from your early experiences, and how are you actualizing those dynamics today? If you feel you have regressed sexually, choose life!

Life yields to time and time to essence and essence to love.

§§§

The Animus

Image: *the hat sits on the table*

"The goal of all projection is integration . . ."

The animus is the masculine energy within a woman. In the love experience we project our dominant's opposite onto the other sex, or onto the opposite within the same sex. A woman generally projects her animus onto a man or onto the animus of another woman. The natural purpose of this type of projection is to get us into relationship so that we may experience and then integrate the projections back within ourselves.

Thus in childhood the young daughter plays out and embodies her father's anima, and he in turn becomes the recipient of his daughter's animus projection. She projects the masculine, and he projects the feminine.

In projection we first see out there what is inside us. It is easier, and usually far more dynamic, to see the strength and decisiveness of the masculine as being in the father rather than being within oneself, especially if the girl is being brought up in frills and lace. If a woman is being educated to identify with the feminine only, the strength of her projected masculine will be correspondingly stronger.

If, however, father is weak in masculine and mother strong in it, then daughter may have a more developed masculine herself. She identifies with her mother and acts strongly. The daughter will react to a weak and passive mother by going against her own feminine and over-developing her masculine side. As an adult she will seek men weaker than herself so that she may never become weak and pathetic like her mother has become.

In the early years the projections need to be lived out. Thus we have the first early love experiences, the crushes on the same sex or opposite sex teachers and onto various friends. You can get a good idea of what your animus was, and perhaps still is, by looking at the qualities of the receivers of your animus projection.

For some young women, their first love is a horse, the magnificent and noble animal whom they learn to tame in order to run freely with. Relating to an actual man comes later. We all know the story of the sophisticated young lady whose first sexual experience was with the groom in the hay of the stable on a rainy afternoon. They rutted like the animals they were because the archetypes, the great energies, were at work.

The young man in childhood also tries to embody the masculine by identifying with it. How he dresses, his behavior, his accomplishments and swagger, are the young man's attempt to identify with and live out his masculine to attract the opposite sex.

The goal of all projection is integration, whether we achieve it or not. The animus is a wonderful dynamic in a woman, for it gives an edge to her natural feminine, a bite, a reservoir of power which says that she can be competent and decisive in her own right, and achieve her purpose in life without benefit of a man's living it for her.

The Work

• Who did you project your animus onto as a young woman? What were the qualities projected? As a woman, how did your mother's animus affect you? How did your animus evoke your father? How did your animus affect your mother? As a young woman, how did your animus affect the men your own age? How did they influence your animus? As a woman today, how do you relate to your own animus? How do other women or men relate to it?

• As a young man, how did your mother affect your ability to relate to the woman's animus? How did your father influence this same ability? Where are you today in terms of your ability to relate to a woman's animus? How do you do it? What do you do?

We first project what we need to become.

§§§

Father

Image: *light breaks through the clouds*

"Someone has to demonstrate to the child that the world can be effectively handled."

My father was never in heaven, but when on earth, and all the time I knew him, he was special to me. Not only would he cook my meals and take me places when I came home on vacation, but he also was famous, which meant I had some admiration from the other boys. Only, they interpreted it as being rich, and I was actually poor as Ben Franklin's church mouse.

I looked up to my father as a boy, not only because he was taller than me, but because he was always telling me what to do. He seemed to know how the world worked. He would try and help me get along with people and deal with what was apparently going to be a pretty harsh reality when I grew up. In fact, from his view of things, I sometimes wondered if I should grow up. Maybe I wouldn't make it out there? He saw the world as beset with adversarial forces you had to fight against.

I remember one time my mother telling me how my father fell down the elevator shaft. Of course, I could hardly keep from laughing because I always thought my father was invincible. Apparently, in the dark he had assumed the elevator was on his floor when it was not, and he had stepped off into space. He had to walk on crutches for awhile. My mother always said father had courage because he didn't complain about the big things.

Another time both of them were walking home past the drunks and the seamen of lower Manhattan, and on the dark narrow street where they lived a husky drunk tried to drag my mother off by the hair. Oscar pulled in the opposite direction and together they got themselves into their building safely.

When I think of my father, I think of him as someone who could go out into the world with all its terrors and deal with things and be successful. He must have been arrogant as well. When a boy on a sled knocked him down from behind in the snow, I laughed and laughed. My father didn't like it at all. He said I shouldn't laugh at things like that. But I couldn't help myself. I laughed without end, so great was the humor of life suddenly coming in and momentarily tearing you out of your dignified place in the world. It had been done to me by my father and now a little boy had gotten him back.

Within the father archetype resides the primary qualities of relating to the world, acting decisively, doing what is necessary to earn a good living, being effective, being directed towards realizable goals, and having a steady strength. Not all fathers achieve the potential of the role. Many women also have to embody these qualities for their children, especially in a changing world where the roles hardly hold anymore. The roles change but the functions remain. Someone has to demonstrate to the child that the world can be effectively handled.

The Work

• Write a description of your own father, including whatever experiences and characteristics come to mind. Then draw out the significance of your picture. What were the values he embodied?

• Write a description of the ideal father, or the fully rounded father. How much did you have or not have? How does this show up today? How has your experience of your father affected your relations with men?

• For the woman, which men in your life have been like your father, or totally different from your father? How is this significant for you?

• How has your personal experience of father affected your concept of God as father?

• How successful are you in the world? How can you tell?

Success is knowing the laws of reality and using them effectively.

§§§

Dating

Image: *the fingers touch while on the grass rests a butterfly*

"We test ourselves in life."

In dating we learn to develop friendships, we learn to play together, to kiss, to caress, to make love, to argue, to help each other out, to be intimate. We all seem to want a daily companion by our side and so we must get out there in the real world and keep meeting people until the right one clicks. In our teenage years we became concerned about our bodies, how we looked, and our social skills. We wanted to be liked. We wanted to have friends. We were afraid of rejection, often having already suffered a severe rejection within our original family. The hormones urged us out. The fears kept us in.

In this contemporary society where major relationships may change every few years, the phenomena of dating still has relevance. Imagine your major relationship has ended and you have been out of circulation for awhile. What do you do? Where are the people who would make good companions? And how do you go about attracting and keeping the right one? How many prospects do you have to date and sleep with until you find the match for you? Generally expect to date ten people to find the next right one for you. Why this number? It means keep dating until the right one meshes with you. Don't try and make the first relationships be the ultimate one.

It cannot be hard to imagine what it must be like to enter the dating arena for the first time. How is it done? How do I handle my emotions, as well as relate to the other person's? What will make me attractive and interesting? What will hold the relationship together? Should it be held together?

Our purpose is to explore those first times to understand them more clearly and accept them so we can evaluate our present performance in the relational game.

Entering the dating arena we replace innocence with the ability to get involved and uninvolved in relationships. We test our effectiveness in our ability to bring a significant someone into our orbit to love. We test ourselves in life. We use all our resources, our psychological awareness and our ability to love. Remembering once again that in loving our contemporaries we are still working through childhood problems first projected onto our parents and then onto significant others.

Everyone can find a mate, which is not based on how naturally beautiful you are. A beautiful and vital personality can be developed which will make even your physical appearance attractive. If you are not seeking or bringing to you good possibilities for relationship check out whether your "standards" are too high, thus denying opportunities there in reality. And check out also whether you are "lovable." Do you love to love, do you love life, and ultimately, do you love yourself? No one loves a loser. Everyone loves someone who loves. To be loved, love!

The Work

• What does the above exposition seem to be saying to you? Make a list of questions or issues evoked by the material in relation to your dating experience.

• As a teenager what were the questions you asked yourself about dating? What was your focus?

• What was your dating or relating pattern as a teenager and young adult? What is your pattern today? What is the evolvement or transformation?

• How much of your inner thoughts do you share with your partner? Why? What is the value in sharing and not sharing?

• What is the secret to successful dating or relating?

• If you are in a long term relationship, do you use your relationship as a safe place to hide, avoiding interactions of the sexes? Or do you still live all your interactions fully?

• What do you think your partner is doing with his or her secret life regarding the masculine and feminine and the sexes? It does not have to be overt. Whatever happens in fantasy and the heart is also real.

• How realistic are you about the relations between the sexes? What are the lessons in this complicated interplay?

Wear your troubles on the outside and no one will see your heart.

§§§

Incest

Image: *the flower is lost in the whirlpool*

"Healing childhood is a large order served at the restaurant of the gods."

It may seem shocking, but it is a psychological fact that most people in their adult life create psychological incest. We marry our parents. We seek out our parents in adult lovers in an attempt to heal the childhood wound, the wound that says we were hurt by a cold and critical parent, or an absent parent, perhaps an alcoholic or abusive parent. We seek to mate with someone who fits the parental description in an attempt this time to transform the "parental personality" through love.

It never works. We receive some healing in the nurturing which sex and companionship bring, but we do not solve the parental problem deep in our psyche. It is only within the myth of childhood that you can heal the wounded child by healing the parental archetypes. We must work on our complexes directly and not expect our friends and lovers to heal us.

In this sense almost all couples need relationship counseling to learn to communicate and process openly, to see what is being projected onto each other which really belongs to the myth of childhood.

We can get over psychological incest, but it may take years. Recognize that you are mating with a parent, someone you want to take care of you, and you will be more cautious and sensitive to the issues. Being unconscious has its advantages. Better not to know whom you are really mating with. You might turn off. In point of fact many couples do turn off to each other sexually and affectionately. Incest goes against nature and they begin to realize that they do not want to sleep with their parents. They want a real companion who does not evoke the childhood mess. They want to mate with someone who does not try to make them a child.

Even though physical incest seems more horrible than psychological incest, it can be worked with as well. Redemption will take place if the parties involved go through dealing with the experience without repressing. Physical incest is unhealthy primarily because it bonds the person to the parent in archetypal ways which are regressive and invasive. Sexual bonding with parents limits the possibility of bonding with one's contemporaries. Many parents may also practice physical incest without actually having overt sex with their children. Certain physical caresses may seem borderline, but it is the seductiveness of the parents which is most damaging. If the parent attempts to keep the teenager bonded to him or her, this borders on physical and psychological incest. The youth needs to break away and find mates outside the family. The original childhood family should no longer come first.

Let your children go. And children, free yourself. For the world is a much bigger place than your family arena can ever be. The world family needs you more than your childhood family has the right to demand or ask for.

Parents who practice open and non-seductive bonding with their children are giving them experiences of human warmth which will enable them to bond freely with others. The love you give your children must be a gift, not an obligation, so they can give it to others. Love is an outward spiral, not an inverted loop ending up in an impossible knot.

The Work

• How have you psychologically slept with your mother or father in your life? What were the good points and the awful feelings associated with the experience? How have you begun to experience redemption of this pattern?

• What commitment will you make to break the "mating with parents" syndrome and find your true mate, the one who is like you rather than like your parents?

When we're not free to bond we cannot bond to get free.

§§§

Work

Image: *the rope has caught the snake's head*

". . . doing what you are creatively best at doing."

In graduating from high school we were ready to go out into the adult world and work, earn a living, practice our survival skills. Perhaps we married instead, or went to college, or traveled. But eventually work would come upon us. We would have to create money in order to live. We would have to find a structure for our lives.

Who likes to work? Retirement is looked forward to by many in this culture as the time when the person can do what he or she wants. But the young must put in their toil and sweat, they must take the best part of the day to labor. The young do the routine labor of the civilization, along with older people who have lost or never developed their full usefulness.

Many slot themselves into a job where they can advance to more responsibility and greater earning power, but the best goal of the work life is to know reality in such a way that you make your work your most individuated and creative endeavor. You make money and contribute to society doing what you are meaningfully best at doing.

To get to the arena of the creative often takes an apprenticeship in routine study and tasks which undergird so much of the advanced work of life. To be the best you must go through the worst. How we were trained in the routine jobs of childhood either helps or hinders us from choosing what is necessary to move ahead in adult life. Pray that your family made you do what you did not want to do as a child so that you may be equipped for the reality of mature life.

Retirement is often the refuge of the burned out who have chosen to fit themselves into a work system which was not that fulfilling. You know that you have found your own destined and creative work if you never retire from it as long as you are able to be effective. Retired people can return to the creative part of childhood and start new careers which express more their talent and passion. The choice is not to go to rest but to new activity. This will keep one passionate as long as one lives.

Most of us do not want a boring job. We want to work in an area where we can express who we are, our values, abilities and passion for life. We like to believe in what we are doing as beneficial to the world. We like to feel that if we put a lot of creative effort in what we do, it will make our job more lasting.

We may also want to make good money so that we can do things beyond merely surviving. We may want to climb the ranks, to move up the ladder according to our efforts and abilities. We may be reaching for more and more responsive situations for our drive.

But so much comes down to attitude and self-image. Do I work for myself, or for others? Am I willing to do the disciplined routine work as well as the creative and new? Is my goal money or satisfaction in The Work?

And on the metaphysical level, am I open to obtaining the prosperity and fulfillment which is there for me in life? Do I complain about my lot, or do I make choices which change things and manifest new possibilities?

The major defeat takes place within our own head. Reality has both the potential for destruction and for fullness. Which I go for depends on my attitude and self-image. A negative self-image is poverty itself. It is so easy to enjoy the results of one's labor rather than complain over what one has not got. Do I bring defeat or accomplishment into my life?

The big challenge in graduating from childhood is to go to work, to work at what you are meant to do in life, to risk and not play it too safe within the nest. If your motivation is security you will forever fail at dealing with fear, you will miss opportunities, and no amount of money will make you feel safe or happy. To work at risk is to live at the edge where the action is, to go for the new opportunity and actualize yourself in a changing world.

The Work

• Describe your childhood attitudes and practices regarding work. Were you successful and praised, or criticized and ignored? What pattern and attitudes were created for you around work and productive fulfillment? Write out a plan to change this now, today, and forever. Seek whatever help is available to change yourself so that you can accomplish fulfillment in work.

• Even if you are secure in a job and in your life's work, there may be areas of new fullness for you. What then are your job-related values and attitudes? What stands in the way of maximizing your potential?

• What exactly is work for you?

When you work for the soul the soul will work for you.

§§§

The Persona

Image: *the painter's canvas is blank*

"But nothing much gets revealed when we reveal the obvious."

Everyone needs a persona to get along in the world. Quite simply, we do not walk naked in most public places. Our persona will prevent us from doing such a thing. Shame and embarrassment are feelings peculiar to an ego identified with the persona, the good and safe side of the personality. We are not our personas, except when we identify with them, which is often.

But even if we walked around naked not much would get revealed. The next barrier would still remain, the next inhibition to absolute freedom would still exist. People can see all of us as they did when we were babies and yet we will remain hidden from them if we choose to hide behind the mask of who we present to the world.

As children we are first groomed by our parents, then we start grooming ourselves, making our body look presentable, neat, and even beautiful according to collective values. Along with the grooming we are taught what to say and not to say to others. We are being educated in correct speech and correct behavior. We identify with the good parts and seek to carefully hide the bad. What attitudes about what is right do we still live out as adults? What is the way to dress, and for whom? What is the appropriate way to act in various situations?

Who is there who has not in their childhood stolen something from someone else? If you have not, why not? Chances are the completely above-board personality is a rigid one. If you identify with your persona, you will create just as big a shadow which those close to you will see and you yourself will be blind to.

The persona itself needs to be related to rather than identified with. My persona is the various roles I play out in the world in order to be effective in it. I can embody certain collective values and stay within the limits of the current trends. I can play the game. We get paid for our personas. I must look and act effective in what I do so that others will value and pay me for my services.

We develop and complete the persona for each stage of life. The first years of my life I played the good child or the bad child. One role got love and the other got blame and deprecation. I soon learned that in order to receive love and caring I had to be good. Then as I left childhood I adopted the behavior and role models of my contemporaries. I made my persona appropriate to my age and culture. I became effective in the world.

The Work

• Is your persona appropriate to your present stage in life? If not, what will you do about it? Evaluate whether you have been affecting a persona beyond your years.

• What was your persona like as a teenager? How is it different now?

• What is my positive image of myself? What is the image others have of me? How do the two images compare?

• How would I like to be seen in the world?

To be seen, put on a mask.

§§§

The Shadow

Image: *the tree falls over on the giraffe eating from its branches*

"The new path is one of increasing emotional honesty..."

I remember visiting my parents as a child and wondering about their hidden lives. I somehow knew that my mother only revealed certain things about herself and my father. How I longed to know all about their lives, but as I was reminded that there were certain things you just didn't talk about.

When I opened the large black trunk after my father's death I found certain objects from my mother's life which I know my father would never have told me about. I hesitate even now to describe some of what was in that trunk, so frail at times seems the human condition.

I found it somewhat pathetic to find my mother's typewriter with a page still in the paper roller where she had typed over and over again,

I am a genius
I am a genius
I am a genius

When alive this crazy part of her must have been trying to evoke a genius quality to produce great poetry. It was an act not to be revealed to anybody.

Also in that trunk I found some paper tissue with dried, yellow, sputum, obviously coughed up from my mother's throat as she lay dying. Such was the shock of her going that my father in his desperation tried to preserve anything he could. He had labeled this bit of uselessness,

"The sputum of the late poet, Gene Derwood."

I am disclosing something meant to be kept hidden. I am disclosing my parents' shadow. People do strange things when their shadow pops out. Normally my father seemed as sane and rational as anyone, but the shock of his grief triggered his shadow, producing an extreme act of intense feeling. Normally my father was a tight, self-contained man with a good wit. This was his persona. He did not have much feeling expression. Feeling was in his shadow, and so it came out in unusual ways.

All of us have a shadow, the repository of the repressed and unlived life. In it we place what others do not like about us and what we also dislike in ourselves. We build our persona, the acceptable side, by repressing the unacceptable. I grew up believing I was a pacifist. I felt contempt for violent people. In therapy I learned to my chagrin that I could be aggressive and violent, that I had a lot of anger inside. I had grown up building a persona of being a nice child to escape punishment. In doing so I had repressed my shadow, my dark, violent side, and had projected it onto others.

In adult intimate life our shadows come out in full swing to plague our partners. You may love each other dearly, but if your shadows are incompatible, you will not be able to live together without repressing.

We need to redeem our shadows and find appropriate ways of expression for them. It is true that we cannot simply express negativity all over the place. We can learn in our adult intimate relations how to express rather than repress the creative energy of the shadow. The new path is one of increasing emotional honesty in which we accept more of ourselves, including the shadow, and find ways of expressing these vital forces of life.

The Work

• Describe what you know of your parents' shadows and the behavior they used to repress their shadows. Then see how their shadow pattern affects you. What was unacceptable in your family? What parts of yourself do you feel were repressed or neglected? Which of these parts have stayed repressed in you? And what can you do about their expression now?

• Choose to discuss with your intimate partner how the shadow pops out or needs expression. Design play forms for expressing each others shadow. This can be in sexuality, play fighting, fantasy enactments, role playing.

• Bring up ways to contain, but not repress, your shadow. Containment is the conscious choice to set boundaries for how energy gets expressed.

The ego has forgotten what the shadow knows.

§§§

Decisiveness

Image: *the jeweler works the gem*

"To be decisive is the ability to act clearly in achieving an immediate goal . . ."

Every archetypal energy can be turned into a function. One of the chief functions of the integrated animus is decisiveness. Both sexes need this quality abundantly to deal with the realities of life on this earth. Were you ever taught how to be decisive and its value?

To be decisive is the ability to act clearly in achieving an immediate goal when that becomes appropriate and necessary. The preparation, the buildup, the letting go, the waiting, all these have their place. But at some point, in the interface with life, we can choose to abandon all hesitation and consideration and act fully with all the power and direction at our command.

In your childhood, who was decisive in the family ? Who was decisive at school? Did you see or learn this as a positive quality? Are there any problems or attitudes from childhood limiting your ability to be decisive? Yes, of course there are, if you are like the rest of us. But in adult life we often need to make strong decisions and stand for a clear direction into the future. It will probably cause pain to ourselves and others, but choosing strongly will also cause changes in the real world and form a base from which to live the next aspect of life.

I can be effective in spite of myself.

The Work

• Where was decisiveness or lack of decisiveness in your childhood, and what effect did it have on you?

• Enter into a period of meditation with your eyes closed and visualize a situation in which you need to become decisive. Allow also images to come which seem to prevent decisiveness. Then see yourself becoming decisive in the situation and note what results.

• How would your life change if you were to become more decisive?

Act when the moment is ripe.

§§§

Fairness

Image: *an old man cracks eggs at the dinner table*

"You did the right thing and you were rewarded."

Most of us had a childhood in which we did not always get what we wanted. A childhood where doing the right thing was not always rewarded,
where others acted out their own destructiveness and often seemed to
obtain the goodies of life anyway. We might have been too honest, too
kind, too considerate of others, and someone else took advantage of this
and did us in to meet their own needs. We protested. We got upset. Even if
we never said a thing in our own defense we secretly protested reality, we
secretly thought that what was done to us was wrong.

As we were growing up we did not like the true stories we heard about
people murdering each other and about the wars going on in the world.
But our complaint was against our parents. Too often they insisted on
getting their way with us. Too often they insisted on their views being the
correct ones. We rebelled, either openly or inside ourselves. Life seemed
unfair and we did not want to be here. We retreated into the realm of fantasy, or began acting out.

School seemed fair most of the time. If we studied and didn't make
disturbances we would receive good grades. We did the right thing and we
were rewarded. We were, unfortunately, being taught a false view of
reality. There is no certain evidence that the just, the good, the ethical,
receive greater benefits for their behavior than the conniving, the
underhanded, the politicians, the power-brokers, the business sharks.

Everyone seems to receive some of life's plenty whether they are
particularly good or not.

So rather than a Judge of Fairness, there may well be in this life a swing
and sway of opposites. It is possible that everyone receives good and bad
in equal measure no matter how good they try to be. Is this fair? It is not
fair but it is balanced.

To integrate the childhood experience the second time around means to accept as a valid part of life the wrongs, the unfairness, which was done to us. To be abused, to lose a parent, to go through emotional or physical hell, shows the dark side balancing the times of health, being well parented, being emotionally sound. Your ego is biased towards the positive. Watch it! What you neglect will take you over.

If we insist that things should be different than they are, we will create false reality pictures and do ourselves in. No absolute fairness exists in life, simply reality and its consequences. No perfect universe exists other than the one we've got. If we build another one in our mind we will weaken our reality sense.

Some people become cynics and go for what they can get. Others appeal to saviors and parental figures to protect them from life. Still others act out of their inner victim to attract healing. The more conscious people accept good and evil as natural forces and seek to meld them into one whole. They redeem their childhoods by realizing that whatever happened is consistent with the way the world works, and if they had a hard childhood they were not that prepared to deal with adversity. The more conscious expect opposites to occur and make realistic plans and processes for coping with both the light and the dark.

Wholeness means expressing all sides of oneself. We need to be consciously bad sometimes, to actualize that energy in life. Try not to be a victim of your own one-sidedness. Those who want only good bring evil upon themselves. This is the great law of opposites. In place of the fairness doctrine put the law of balancing the opposites by honoring and integrating both sides. If we substitute objectivity for fairness, life will go better for us.

The Work

• What is your earliest memory or experience of the world not being fair, and what kind of reaction did that realization produce in you?

• If you still expect people and situations to be fair, describe your own attitudes which might be producing this expectation.

• Are you using all the power available to you in your life? If not, what attitudes may be blocking your living to the fullest.

Balancing opposites brings healing.

§§§

Forgiveness

Image: *open hands cup the blood*

"We are our own worst adversary, and that is where the issue of forgiveness lies."

I know that for most of us there is someone back there in the early years who hurt us, and whom we do not want to forgive.

Although my parents gave me a hellish childhood, I can see purpose and gentleness looking back at their actions. Perhaps their decision of sending me away at age six wasn't so bad. Would it have been any better living with them instead of living at boarding school? My wrath is more for the military school teacher who suddenly yanked me out of my seat and started beating me furiously about my head. But what is there to forgive about such evil?

What is there to forgive for all the world's murderers and soldiers who kill without decency? Many of us who have been victims would rather fight back and kill our adversaries. But there are so many adversaries in this life. If we could kill them all, who would be left?

We are our own worst adversary, and that is where the issue of forgiveness lies. If I focus on the one I hate, the one in whom I see no possibility for redemption, then I will never be able to forgive. If I focus on myself, then the possibility is there to let go of the past, no matter what it has been.

We do not forgive in the sense of absolving someone of a wrong doing. Forgiveness is an act of sacrifice, an act of letting go of what has already been taken from us. Those who cannot forgive are still holding on to what should have been. What was, is reality. What should have been never exists.

We let go of the past to be more fully in the present. Forgiveness is redemption for myself, not another. Perhaps the energy will change with the adversary also, but that is not within our control.

The process of forgiveness is to recall and experience the wounds you received and who caused them. To feel what happened as a necessity. We do not forgive through will power. We can only forgive when we cannot forgive. There must be sacrifice. I must own what I am letting go of. In most cases of resentment against parents it is not necessary to encounter the actual parents. The parents of today are not the parents of your childhood. The process of forgiveness is an inner process of experiencing and letting go of the defensiveness around your own wounds. We let go of seeing the world as one great adversary with others to blame for our own misfortune.

You are in fear of life until you can forgive. Remaining in old wounds at some point becomes indulgence, becomes remaining identified with the Victim. To free yourself from the Adversary through forgiveness is to free yourself from identification with the Victim Archetype.

Perhaps light a candle, list the wrongs created by your adversaries, let yourself feel them without any longer being defensive about them, and then let go completely. Let go of the adversary and let go of being a victim. You may write a letter to your inner child or to your inner parents. And be in a sacred space where you cannot be disturbed and can experience healing, such as in nature or a place of meditation.

For myself, a few years ago in analysis I made my mother's head in clay and when the impulse came to me I destroyed it. What was wiped out in that piece of clay was her hold on me. Once I allowed expression of the worst I could go on to better. She became a fallible human being to me, not so much my mother anymore. My new mother was alive inside me as I grew in feeling and expressed my nurturing and birthing side in my life.

The Work

• From what is described in the above text, create a procedure for yourself to forgive the adversaries of childhood. Perhaps you do not feel ready, or will have to do it more than once. Are we ever fully ready for the next step? Go through your process, either alone or with others, and write about what comes up.

• If you have not been able yet to go through the process of forgiveness, then list what is stopping you and look for healing dreams and experiences.

• "Forgive us our destructive acts as we forgive those who have been destructive towards us." comes from a well known religious text. Where does forgiveness come from according to this teaching? Is forgiveness, or redemption, a given as part of the universe or an act which comes from an arbitrary deity which must be importuned? What must we do? What must the source of forgiveness do? In order to be forgiven, or feel redeemed of past wounds, blocks, and even deliberate acts of evil or destructiveness, what must we do? The choice is to do what?

• Is there anything in life which a person cannot be forgiven for? On what basis? Is there always healing for every conflict or act of destructiveness?

• Now work on redeeming childhood by going through a forgiveness process, the rage, the hurt, the helplessness, the defensiveness which occurred as a result, the letting go of defensiveness and blocks, the choice to be freed of the past, the felt coming in of a healing power from other than ego, the shift in life perspective or world view, the commitment to living a new and transforming life.

Those who forgive little will gain little.

§§§

Choice-Making

Image: *lightning breaks out on a clear day*

"We say Yes to one thing and No to all that would oppose it."

I remember years ago visiting a friend of mine. Bedtime for their three year old came and they presented the child with choices. "Do you want to go to bed now? Do you want a story read to you? Do you want some hot chocolate? Do you want your red pajamas?" I hate to list the several more questions they asked their three year old. Finally he said, "No, no, no, no, no!" to everything. The "good" parents had overwhelmed their child with choices. They had tried to dump their own choice-making responsibility onto a child who was not at that level yet. They did not know the power and nature of choice-making. Nor did they realize that choosing against is not the same as choosing for something.

Choice-making appears to be one of the most neglected areas of life. Where are the courses and books on the subject? Every day of our lives we make choices, yet how many of us have the skills for this activity?

One key to effectiveness is the ability to make choices. A choice is putting energy in one direction and not another. We say Yes to one thing and No to all that would oppose it.

Many of us are more attracted to saying Yes than No, and then after awhile all the Yeses we have said overwhelm us. Stress comes from having said Yes without saying No. Fewer people say No more often than Yes in life. Saying No can be creative if in saying No we are opening ourselves to the possibility of saying Yes. Better to say No than an automatic Yes which we do not carry out.

But there are those, very guarded perhaps, who mostly say No or say nothing. The No-sayers may need to be more open to life's possibilities and risk more. If caught in a bind and ambivalence, start choosing, saying Yes to things over and over again. Such a practice will break the pattern and give you plenty of consequences to deal with.

Perhaps you feel that the Universe is always saying No to you and therefore you must protect yourself by also saying No to the Universe? Who will break this cycle first? You or the Universe? You have the power of choice, you break the pattern first!

Somewhere around age seventeen many of us begin making our own choices as to how to live our lives. We are still dependent, yet want to be independent. We know that within a year or two we will be more or less out on our own in life. We no longer take the parents' opinions as the right opinions about life. We rebel, or go against. We want to make our own choices. This is the birth of the creative ego in the seventeen year old, the birth of a distinct personality willing to go against the parents to find him or herself. Choice in this case is the demarcation line between self-identity and family expectations.

Many of us who did not develop creative ego in the late teens, as adults learn to have our own perceptions and opinions, and to make our own choices. We learn to take the consequences regardless of what others say. No one can make your choices for you. You sink or swim yourself.

The Work

When did you start making choices for yourself? Describe the dynamics and what you learned about life from the experience. Perhaps the first ones were more in the No category? Perhaps there were some great Yes choices, say regarding love relationships? What were the consequences and how did you deal or not deal with them? Did you feel you got burned, that you were not ready for choice? How has your high school experience colored your attitudes towards choices and their consequences?

• What are some of the major choices you are needing to make at the present time. What is your choice-making process? Your underlying attitudes? The alternatives in the situation? What you like and dislike? The greatest potential and value in the situation? The sense of appropriate timing? The larger perspective? The specific immediate choices needing to be made? Your commitment to dealing with the consequences?

• Write out a procedure for choice-making beginning to end.

What we choose is what we become.

§§§

Graduating From School

Image: *the vase of old flowers is thrown into the air*

"To graduate is to close the door to the past and take only the essence with you."

Graduation at last! We are going out into the world. The tune, "Pomp and Circumstance," runs through my ears. I experience transcendence and joyful sadness. As a march, it moves me forward in life. As a feeling experience, it allows me to look backwards for the last time.

Up until now we have been part of a family and peer group. At graduation we go out into the world as an individual to find our own friends and way of life. Some of us will stay close to home and the familiar habits we have known. Others will go even thousands of miles away into different life styles. This is the parting of the ways. To celebrate is to honor the transition. We are being required by the prod of time to move on.

Turn and look forward now. The future we must anticipate. The future is always wherein life lies.

Will I let go of the past? Will I embrace the transition despite fears? Do I have a sense of the heroic? Have I taken stock of myself and my ability to interact in the world?

Graduation. It happens every so often in life. A major job or relationship ends. Have I gotten the teaching, or am I upset because of all the missed opportunities? To graduate is to close the door to the past and take only the essence with us. Its lesson is how to let go so that we can open ourselves to the future.

How we graduate affects all the other transitions in our lives. If we never leave childhood we will have a hard time accepting the next turning points on the way. Moving to another place or city, making a marriage and a family, welcoming the birth of a child without too much regret or fear, choosing meaningful work, committing to the spiritual journey, dealing with children leaving home, making a major vocation change, accepting severe illness, experiencing the peak of one's life and career, dealing with dying and death, these are all major transitions affected by how we did or did not leave childhood. Leaving childhood is the first great transition. If we did not go through a sufficient initiation process into life, in all the subsequent transitions we will be reliving the original attempt at graduating into life, including the fears and resistances we hardly dealt with the first time around. Better to finally graduate than to hang on forever fearful of the next stages in life.

Let us celebrate all the stages of life!

The Work

• Write up your graduation experience as it was for you. Then write it as you would have liked it to have been.

• These are the essentials of the graduation experience:
• Anticipating the new, the next stage in life
• Wanting to regress, to stay on at the present stage or even go backwards to an earlier time in your life
• Honoring what has been by bringing it to essence
• Honor through recall who you were, where you started, and how far you have come
• Feeling afraid of the future, the dangers, the new
• Sensing the grand adventure of moving into new life
• Practicing self-definition
• Listing one's skills, personality characteristics, and accomplishments so far in life
• Formalizing the transition with self-reflection, ceremony and celebration with friends and significant others
• Choosing new life
• Dealing with the common side of life which will come after to ground you again in the everyday tasks of life.

• If you have been to any class reunions, what feelings and issues were evoked for you? How have you grown?

• What are your attitudes toward transition and renewal? Which ones need changing? What are some new affirmations or attitudes which you would like to practice around this theme?

• Much additional suffering is caused by resistance to change. How does this dynamic affect your life?

• What do you need to graduate from at the present time?

For the living there is no death, only transition.

§§§

Compromise With Reality

Image: *the black king snake suns himself on a large rock*

"This good earth is the arena of the real."

Let's face it. Many of us do not at times want to be here. Reality seems a difficult if not horrible place to exist. The stresses and strains get us down. We have major gifts, great thoughts, but we don't quite seem to make it in this world. We wish it were simpler. Perhaps if we were more hardy, more intelligent, not who we are, things would go better? Maybe if we hadn't had the difficult childhood we had, the parents we had, it would go better?

But we are in the present moment. We live with this reality, whatever the handicaps. One person is sick much of the time, allergic to this and to that. Another has been afflicted with amenorrhea, the inability to menstruate, and feels handicapped as a woman. Someone else is born into a wealthy family and feels neglected enough to consider suicide. A child who dreamed over and over again of being on crutches following Jesus later developed polio, was confined to a wheelchair, and became a nun. Some hide out in their rooms as children. Others escape the house of tension whenever they can. Still others are beaten, sexually molested, not understood. Reality hurts, and sometimes hurts badly.

Do we want to be here? Is the adult life, where we hope to have more choice, any more free and fulfilling than a rough childhood?

The way out is the way through. This life of ours is the arena of the possible, the one place to be. Be here now. If you can give up your idealism, your longing, your values which are too high, your compulsive fears, then you have a chance to live a fulfilling life. But you must choose to be here. Make as strong a choice as you can to create your choices within the arena of the possible. The preliminary requirement for making this great choice is to have acknowledged and worked through the central aspects of your childhood.

Yes, make your compromise with reality. You will know those who have made a similar commitment as yours by their human quality. They can look you in the eye. They have a ready response to every moment, every issue. They take joy and suffering alike in equal value. They do not hide behind any trappings, religious, family, work, neurosis, friendship, or the like. They exist as persons in their own right and treat you as an individual capable of a similar consciousness. When you are around such people your own awareness expands and good choices come out of nowhere. You feel the center within the other person and seem to respond naturally from your own center within. There is no complaining. There are only choices and their consequences.

This good earth is the arena of the real. Deal with it. Welcome to reality! Welcome to life!

The Work

• Why not continue to resist the real? List the ways you can still resist your life. How can you improve on them, become even more defensive and unreal. Devise a grand plan.

• Describe the defense system you built up in childhood for resisting the way things were. Did you fantasize a different world? Write down your imaginary world. Behind the symbols are the seeds of your future life, the potentials for healing a sick childhood.

• Are you a controller or a fantasizer? Are you selecting certain segments of your life and repressing others you fear? Go where the fear is, there you will find the ego dangerously close to non-acceptance of reality. Change your attitude at the fear place. Begin the new approach with "I accept things just as they are and I will . . . ."

• When you are almost ready devise a simple ceremony or meditation which indicates your choice to enter fully into this world as it truly is. This is your compromise with reality, this is your grand choice to be as real as you can. Perhaps your choice might include the following elements.

•• I will live as fully as I can in the present moments as they come.

•• I will attempt not to space out into the past or the future as I make my daily choices.

•• I choose to be here. This is the arena of my life to be lived now. I am choosing to be alive to each moment as it comes. I will find my fulfillment in the potentials which come my way, not in fantasies or other forms of unconsciousness.

•• I will work not to repress unpleasant experiences, but to process them with an ongoing commitment to wholeness. I want to be fully alive, and to participate passionately in the world.

•• I will gradually cease those destructive practices which make me go unconscious as an avoidance of reality. Any substance which alters my perception of reality as it is and weakens my ability to choose at an everyday level is likely to be destructive to my choice-making.

•• I will live passionately including life's opposites. I will not leave out the dark side. I am alive now, and that is what counts.

Reality heals us as it wounds us!

§§§

The Letter

Dear people in my childhood,

My mother, Gene Derwood, my father, Oscar Williams, Richard and Diana, brother and sister friends of mine, Miss Day, my best teacher, and all the other supportive teachers and friends.

I needed you, and perhaps you needed me. Parents chose not to raise me and so I respond to all of you.

This is a letter of good-by to the good and the bad. I have returned to childhood to experience and process what was there. Now I let it go. I give up the traumas and resentments. I laugh at them. They did not do me in and I am now very much alive. True, I still have bouts of sickness, nausea just like in childhood. I am having a severe bout right now. I am amazed at how much suffering I can take. And I also look forward to healthier times. I don't ever expect to be completely cured of childhood. That would be perfection. I am willing to live the suffering which comes my way.

And what have I gained from childhood which I take with me? My ruggedness, my ability to persist despite all odds. A devotion to healing in God, in myself and in others. God, or Source, seems to have much darkness and imperfection. How else can I explain the bad stuff which happened to me. Why should I exclude anything?

Time once again to move on. I have been there and returned, hopefully with more compassion and consciousness this round. And I thank others who have traveled with me. We have journeyed into and out of childhood together.

My love, my parents, my children, my friends and enemies, are alive in me. I shall sign this letter with all of the names of my heritage. Good-bye!

-Strephon Derwood Kaplan-Williams

Graduating From Childhood

Image: *receiving a black cloth and a golden staff*

"We are here. There is no where else we can possibly be."

What follows must be taken with self-acceptance on all our parts. Do we, can we, in fact graduate from childhood? How we have survived childhood affects deeply the rest of our lives, no matter how much we put ourselves through self-transformation. Yet there are certain fundamentals which can indicate what the real graduation from childhood is like.

The Fundamentals

• A person who has graduated from childhood seldom complains about anything. To complain is to be critical and non-accepting of something without doing anything about it. At the root this complaining is a statement that the complainer's childhood should have been different than it was. Not having accepted childhood exactly as it was means that we still have grounds for complaint. We don't like something and wish it were different. We want things to be other than they are. Furthermore, the true complainer never makes much effort to change the conditions which cause the complaint.

In childhood we were faced with things which caused us pain and we were helpless to do anything about most of them. The adults had the power. The only way we could resist was by crying, pouting, throwing a tantrum. If we didn't develop a strong sense of choice as we grew up, we continued to feel powerless in the face of adversity. We continued to complain. In adult life when opposed we complain. We have awful husbands, governments, world conditions, headaches, and so on. The point is not to complain about any of these conditions but to do something about them. If you feel something is wrong, change it! If you can't change it, change yourself!

And what if you cannot change what you consider an oppressive situation or person? Then accept reality as it is or get out. Why be involved in any situation which you do not have the power to influence or change?

• The mature adult makes his or her compromise with reality. How many of us have accepted being here on earth? Are we still resisting anything in life? It's difficult not to wish for things we don't have. As children we always wished for something better than we got. Now we have entered adult life and we are still wishing for things to be different than they are. We construct in our minds and ideal reality with which to evaluate and flee from the real world. If you are resisting anything in this life you have not yet made your compromise with reality. You still want a better lover than you've got, more money than you have, a different place to live, being a different sex. You name it, somebody has wished for it.

To make our compromise with reality is to work within its confines. We accept what is and create with it. We live in the arena of the possible. We live now, not later. Whatever life we have, we have now. We are here. There is no where else we can possibly be.

• For the mature adult the parents no longer exist as parents. They are people now. The children as adults owe them nothing and are owed nothing. Your parents are the old life. You are moving into the new. Let them be. Let them go. Move on.

Parents have no special rights over their grown children. People will take the most outrageous things from parents which they would never take from their closest friends. The adult child is still afraid of offending the parent because in childhood the parents played the power game and broke their children, instilling fear in them because of their use of power. If you are afraid of offending your parents in any way, shape, or form you have not yet become an adult.

• We choose not to form dependency relationships as places to hide in adult life. In actuality we all form dependency relationships, but these in our modern era often split up with much suffering on both sides.

What happens of course is that the umbilical cord is severed once again in a relationship dissolution. The cord will be severed if it is a dependency relationship. It may be severed anyway. Through sex we establish the umbilical cord to The Mother, our partner of either sex, and when the relationship breaks we cry out, re-experiencing the agony of original loss. In addition to being an instinctual response, wanting sex is wanting re-attachment to The Mother for renewal or regression from adult life. Successfully solving the dependency syndrome means that we are living our own lives in as many ways as we can, including financially, sexually, in friendship, and in personal growth. No longer will the partners play am-ateur therapists to each other, although they will support each other's growth. We relate without attempting to control each other. We meet our own needs, and thereby are more able to support our partner in meeting his or her needs.

• We are committed to working through dependency issues whenever they come up. While we may not be in a dependency relationship, we will have surges of dependency arising from the past or from present stress. We must in these cases take our courage in our hands and support our own growth instead of expecting our partners to meet our needs.

• We do not resist life transitions but celebrate them meaningfully. Because we have made a transition out of childhood in working through our material, we are able to meet and take hold of all the other transitions in life.

The people who have the hardest time dying have never left childhood. They want to stay alive because they never lived. They then have to work through all the dependency issues in dying that they should have worked through years earlier. They experience the archetypal wounded child in their own sickness once again, and finally, they may have numinous experiences of the wondrous child as they die. It seems paradoxical that the dying experience should be a final return to childhood experience, but if you have not grown up of course you must go back to the beginning in order to face your ending.

• We commit to living from the Divine Child archetype, the archetype of the Self. We live a new essence daily. We are spontaneous beings, flexible and resilient to the end of our days. We have vitality and consciousness. A manifestation of spiritual power shows in much of what we do. We have made ourselves a vehicle for a larger process than ego, a larger process than even our parents hoped or expected for us. We do not live out our parents' expectations. We do not live out our own expectations. We live the potentials of the central archetype, parented now by the sources of the universe. We are reborn daily into life. We choose to protect and nurture that new birth through daily action.

• If we have already graduated from childhood we welcome death when it comes as an ultimate experience of transition. We do not fear to die because we have achieved a major adult task, which is to leave childhood dependency behind and finally live from the Divine Child, the central archetype of the Self. Death then becomes an experience of divinity in which we feel ourselves as the child of God, one who has been given the supreme gift of life, realized it, and now exits this world.

You give what you have been given.

§§§

Saying Good-bye

Image: *a pitcher filled with clear water and two glasses*

"But I cannot, I choose not to remain there."

This is our ceremony. The time has come, as time moves on, to leave that first early period of childhood. I have returned there in many ways and been moved by many things. But I choose not to remain there. The future again calls me onward to life. I am to say good-bye. I am to let go of that period of my life as I acknowledge once again who I was and will never again be. Yet in leaving I may take the essence with me, the core of my destiny to live now.

I say good-bye to all that was.

I say good-bye to the small child.

I say good-bye to the parents who loved me and found me difficult.

I say good-bye to the wounds and the joys back then.

I say good-bye to all I did and did not get.

I say good-bye to my little child self.

I see you now. I hug and embrace you. I let go of all that was then because my heart is changing.

I see you, yet I let you go. I must move on.

The Work

• The above ceremonial refrain can to be used as an honoring and a letting go process in order to help bring further resolution to that period of our lives. In our "saying good-bye" ceremony we toast the past, say the child's name, and read the refrain. So now please read over the refrain and use it as a suggestion for writing your own refrain to say at the ceremony. Take it as far as you can, knowing that there is still, and maybe always will be, more early childhood material to work through. Perhaps see the small child you as you write or say the refrain.

• Allow your feelings and images to be present to you. What was once overwhelming can now be cleansing. Feel the support. Feel the family and strength of the adult years. The new sustenance and community are all those who journey with you, who are committed at various levels to developing the inner way and achieving consciousness and wholeness.

In ending, evoke beginning!

§§§

Death-Rebirth

For every season there is a choice.
A time to die and a time to live.
A time for decrease and a time for increase.
For every beginning there is an ending.
A time for regression and a time for growth.
A time for saying good-bye and a time for saying hello.

For anything new the old must go.
A grave to be dug and new seed planted.
A sacrifice made as well as fulfillment created.

The days of our years are numbered by eternity.
What was will never again be.
The songs which have been sung are only an echo.

We are as grains of sand in the infinitude of oceans.
Our consciousness illumines life for only an instant.
We are as nothing in a transcendent now.

And what we have we have not.
What we are we will not be.
What we can become is already
A burden on our shoulders.

Where is my life going? asks the seeker.
To what end are all my choices?
And for what purpose have I been born or unborn?

Yet still will I say my refuge is in what is.
My salvation is in what I do with what life brings me.
My longing is within the sacred.

When I am no more the rains will still fall.
The seasons will swirl into eternity.
And the voice of my lips will be somebody's song.

For I am not alone in my common humanity.
I am not alone in the journey towards wholeness.
I am at peace where the center guides me.
And I shall live in all my dying.

Dreamwork Tapes

1. Remembering and Incubating Dreams:
The basics of remembering dreams and
how to ask your dreams for perspective on
life issues. Side B is a half hour dream incubation meditation. $7.95

2. Dream Reentry: The most powerful healing dreamwork technique of the Jungian-
Senoi approach. Side B is a guided dream
reentry for working with your dream. $7.95

3. Following the Dream Ego: The out-
standing technique for learning about
yourself through dreamwork. Side B takes
you through the actual procedure. $7.95

4. Dream Incubation: How to evoke
dreams on your life issues, and how to
work with them to obtain their meaning.
Side B takes you through a Dream
Incubation while falling asleep. $7.95

5. Dream Enactments: How to act out your
dreams in safe and expressive ways so
that they may become part of your being.
Side B takes you through enacting your
dream. $7.95

6. Dream Amplification (Interpretation):
The art of understanding your dream symbols consciously. Includes a 300 item spo-
ken Symbol Glossary on side B, which is a
learning in itself. $7.95

7. Dreams and Relationship: How to bring
your dreams to relationship to have more
fulfilling relationships. Side B takes you
both through a sharing around a dream.
$7.95

8. Complete Set of Dreamwork Tapes:
Tapes 1 - 7. Seven hours of dreamwork
instruction which will help you understand
dreams and make changes in your life.
$50 per set.

Postage and handling:

Psychology Tapes

9. Transforming Childhood: Strephon's
four talks on the nature of our myth of childhood, how to know it, transform it, and graduate to mature life no matter what age you
are. Complementary to Strephon's book,
Transforming Childhood. Set of four tapes
(around 5 hours) $30

10. Transforming Anger: Four talks by
Kaplan-Williams on this most intense of life
energies, how to deal with it, how to transform anger into the effective life. Worth the
many changes which will come from working
with this material. Set of four tapes (around
5 hours) $30

**11. The Psychological and Spiritual
Teachings of Jesus**-a spiritual and Jungian
approach. Interpreting the historical teachings of Jesus in modern Jungian terms with
insight which applies to all our spiritual jour-
neys. Set of four tapes (5 hours) $30

**12. Letting Go—A Spiritual Induction
Tape:** Designed by Strephon for a wife and
husband team going through giving birth.
The mother played this tape for 14 straight
hours and achieved the greatest experience
of her life. Giving birth consciously enabled
her to live the process on a spiritual as well
as physical level. Highly recommended, not
only for birth, but any letting go experience.
With Tibetan bells. $7.95

13. Transforming Suffering: A warm and
healing talk on dealing with suffering and adversity. Gives methods and attitude changes
needed. Suffering transformed is one of our
greatest achievements. $7.95

14. Sleep: A talk on the nature of sleep as
going into the unconscious. Side B has an
induction for falling asleep. Good for those
having trouble sleeping, and for those wanting to let go to their own unconscious. $7.95

$2.00 for one or more tapes

Journey Press
P.O. BOX 9036
Berkeley, CA 94709